The Innovative Investor
Version 1.0

Excel Templates for Investments

David C. Shimko
V.P., Risk Management Advisory, Bankers Trust Company

Dennis Foster
Foster Communications

Matthew Will
Johns Hopkins University

Irwin
McGraw-Hill

Boston, Massachusetts Burr Ridge, Illinois Dubuque, Iowa
Madison, Wisconsin New York, New York San Francisco, California St. Louis, Missouri

Irwin/McGraw-Hill
A Division of The McGraw-Hill Companies

THE INNOVATIVE INVESTOR VERSION 1.0

1 2 3 4 5 6 7 8 9 0 BBC/BBC 9 0 9 8 7

ISBN 0-256-14634-9

http://www.mhhe.com

Table of Contents

Introduction

The Innovative Investor was produced by Advanced Financial Software, Inc., Los Angeles, CA, in conjunction with McGraw-Hill of Burr Ridge, IL.

The programs are professional in nature, not tutorial. They provide a powerful learning tool flexible enough to adapt to many learning strategies. However, students should know something about the problems they encounter before bringing them to these worksheets for numerical calculations or simulations. While every attempt has been made to make these worksheets user-friendly, the worksheets assume some familiarity with the underlying concepts. This familiarity can be gleaned through patient study of an investments text. In no way should this software be construed as a substitute for a textbook. While it alleviates the computational burden placed upon students in investments courses, it is hoped that the programs can contribute to the development of the student's investment intuition.

The usual limitations apply to the use of this software: neither Advanced Financial Software, Inc., nor McGraw-Hill, accept any liability for damages resulting from the use of these products. No computer calculation, representation, or printout is intended to constitute a recommendation for or against the purchase or sale of actual securities. Therefore, while the programs are professional in nature, they are intended for academic uses.

This packet contains information on uses of *The Innovative Investor* programs. It also contains several intermediate to advanced problem sets for investment students. Solutions to these problems are also provided.

The programs furnished with *The Innovative Investor* take the form of Microsoft Excel worksheets. To use these worksheets, the user must have an IBM-PC or compatible, with Windows 3.1 or Windows 95 and Microsoft Excel version 5.0 or higher.

Special thanks for helpful feedback during the development of The Innovative Investor go to Zvi Bodie, Boston University, Alex Kane, University of California at San Diego, Alan Marcus, Boston College, and Robert McDonald, Northwestern University.

Recognition and thanks for development work in converting these tools to Excel:

Dennis Foster	Foster Communications
Matthew W. Will	Johns Hopkins University
Marty Benson	

And to the people at Irwin/McGraw-Hill

Shelley Kronzek	Associate Sponsoring Editor
Paula M. Krauze	Editorial Assistant
Charles Petto	Qulaity Assurance Analyst

Overview of Worksheets

These worksheets should be used in conjunction with an undergraduate or Master of Business Administration course in investments. The philosophy of the worksheets rests on the following assumptions:

1. The student has read relevant sections of an investments textbook, or seen some material presented in class related to that subject matter.

2. The student has a beginning grasp of these concepts, but may have trouble "seeing the big picture" because of the level of difficulty or tedium involved in some of the calculations.

3. The student has a fundamental curiosity with respect to these models, and wants to establish his intuition. He is willing to experiment with assumptions to see their individual effects upon outcomes, although he might not have the time to perform these calculations manually.

Therefore, you will not see a worksheet calculating the required rate of return on an asset in the CAPM knowing the underlying assumptions; the value-added for a worksheet in this area is quite small. The worksheets included here perform advanced and complicated calculations and present them in logical ways, using tables and graphs.

The worksheets appear professional in nature. They are intended to solve problems, not to take a student by the hand and lead him through a survey of modern investment thought. The programs are not tutorial, although if properly used they will provide a strong learning tool.

The pedagogy comes on strong in these worksheets. You will see this feature in particular when you attempt the problems in the back of this instruction manual. The worksheets were written by David C. Shimko. David C. Shimko was named Vice President in the Risk Management Advisory Group at Bankers Trust in April 1997. Prior to joining Bankers, he was Vice President and Head of Risk Management Research at J.P. Morgan Securities, responsible for ongoing research into strategic and analytical risk management questions for J.P. Morgan and its clients. Prior to coming to Morgan in 1993, Dr. Shimko was Assistant Professor of Finance at the University of Southern California and a private consultant to financial institutions. He has published over 40 academic and trade articles on strategic issues and the practice of risk management. He has produced financial software packages and has written a technical textbook at the Ph.D. level entitled Finance in Continuous Time: A Primer. He writes a monthly end-user column in Risk Magazine. Dr. Shimko completed his Ph.D. in Managerial Economics/Finance from Northwestern University in 1988, and his B.A. in Economics from Northwestern in 1982.

For this edition, Dennis Foster converted the original Lotus 123 sheets to Excel and recreated the Crunch program as an Excel Add-In. Dennis Foster is the owner of Foster Communications, a 17 year old software applications development firm. He holds a B.A. from Azusa Pacific College and a M.Ed. from Xavier University. His recent projects include the design and development of a budgeting system for evaluating publishing projects for the McGraw-Hill Higher Education Group, a shell program for delivering supplemental textbook materials on CD-ROM, and the development of the 1997 CD-ROM version of the 75th edition of *Writer's Market*. His *Interviewing Skills for Dietetic Practitioners* laser disc training program won a nomination for the Mark of Excellence Award from the International Interactive Communications Society. He presented a paper to the Society for Applied Learning Technologies on the object oriented simulation system he developed for electronic maintenance training called OAR.

Matthew W. Will, Johns Hopkins University co-authored the problems for the Excel edition of *The Innovative Investor*. Matthew Will is an instructor of finance at Johns Hopkins University. He holds a B.S. in Actuarial Sciences and a M.B.A. in Finance, both from Indiana University. He served as Coordinator of Research at the "Center for Real Estate Studies," based at Indiana University. In addition to his academic work, Mr. Will has worked in the private sector for both Fortune 500 firms and small regional companies. He currently teaches "Corporate Financial Theory," "Investments Analysis & Portfolio Management," "Advanced Corporate Finance," and "Derivative Securities." Mr. Will received the 1997 "Excellence In Teaching Award" from the Johns Hopkins University Business Division. He also spends time providing consulting services to non-profit and charitable organizations in the areas of finance and technology.

Individual Worksheet & Program Descriptions

Part I Portfolio Management Worksheets

1. The Efficient Portfolio Frontier (effport.xls)

The user provides expected returns, standard deviations, and correlations for a set of up to 10 securities. Alternatively, if the user runs *Crunch* (see p. 12), the data will be read automatically. The program calculates characteristics of various portfolios given these inputs. With or without a riskless asset, the user can select efficient portfolios by target return or risk aversion levels. In all cases full portfolio composition is provided. Graphics show in risk/return coordinates, the location of the assets, the efficient frontier, and the maximum attainable utility level curve.

2. The Super Efficient Portfolio Frontier (supereff.xls)

Modeled after *The Efficient Portfolio Frontier*, this worksheet goes the extra mile. In *The Efficient Portfolio Frontier*, the optimal portfolio holdings are calculated assuming no constraints are placed on the investor. In *The Super Efficient Portfolio Frontier*, the investor may impose positivity constraints (i.e., no short sales) and up to eight inequality or equality constraints on the portfolio. The optimal portfolio holdings are calculated for any constraint set, and the results are compared to the unconstrained case.

3. Index Models & Performance (index.xls)

This worksheet reads data from *Crunch*, or can use data supplied by the user. The security market line is estimated, and the position of the securities relative to the SML is shown. If the individual securities are in fact mutual funds themselves, this worksheet can be used to calculate the performance of the funds using four different measures and rank the funds accordingly.

Part II Bond & Valuation Worksheets

4. Bond Risk Analysis (bondrisk.xls)

This program determines duration, modified duration, and convexity from quoted bond prices. It can also calculate prices from given yields. The user can specify three portfolios for comparative analysis. The program analyzes profit and loss on the three portfolios, and automatically determines duration matching and convexity-matching strategies. Graphical displays and automated print procedures are included.

5. Term Structure (termstr.xls)

The user provides newspaper quotes for up to 12 bond prices (with or without accrued interest), and gives exact dates of reference (e.g., today) and maturity. Using novel techniques, the program determines duration, volatility, and yield for each of the bonds. The user can then plot a yield curve (term and yield) or a duration/yield profile (similar to a term structure), and use either profile to value securities with arbitrary cash flows. The program determines required yields on individual cash flows by linearly interpolating the points the user provides. For cash flows beyond the range of term or durations of given bonds, the program assumes the yield curve constant.

6. Quick Bond Valuation (quikbond.xls)

This worksheet calculates bond prices, duration and convexity from a collection of input values. The calculations can be reversed to find the implied yield, implied coupon for a bond sold at par, and any other implied calculations. The worksheet includes full What-if and graphics capabilities.

Differences between *Bond Risk Analysis*, *Term Structure* and *Quick Bond Valuation*

While the data formats of these three worksheets are similar, they perform three distinct functions. *Term Structure* uses bond prices to calculate the term structure, while calculating duration and convexity for the sake of convenience. *Bond Risk Analysis* takes the duration and convexity calculations to their logical conclusion – an application of duration and convexity matching in bond portfolio management. *Quick Bond Valuation* is a simple bond calculator program that can also compute duration and convexity and show comparative statics. *Quick Bond Valuation* uses a single bond, and does not allow newspaper-type reporting conventions.

7. Valuing Convertible Debt (convpric.xls)
Using Ingersoll's assumptions and methods (see the program for details), the worksheet calculates values of straight debt, callable debt, convertible debt, and callable-convertible debt for a given financial scenario. The user can provide underlying data, note the effect of changes in financial position on the values of these securities, and study the optimal call and conversion policies for the bonds. The worksheet provides interpretative help and suggested problems for solution. Finally, the user can graph the relative values of the four bonds, or graph the bondholders' gains resulting from inefficient call policies.

8. The Two-Dividend Growth Model (twodiv.xls)
Based on a two-stage dividend growth model, this worksheet determines share value by discounting dividends at a required rate of return. The user may either solve for the value of the equity, or provide an estimate of its value and learn what discount rate was applied to determine that value. Alternatively, whenever four variables are supplied the program calculates the missing variable. In some cases, this comes from closed form solutions, but for two cases Newton-Raphson iterative methods are used to find the missing variables. The user can automatically produce What-if tables from the worksheet. Users can access real balance sheet data for 100 companies to use in the worksheet.

Part III Futures & Options Worksheets

9. Futures Valuation and Risk Management (futures.xls)
This is an easy-to-use worksheet to price futures contracts using the cost-of-carry relationships. Strategies involving up to three futures contracts on a single underlying commodity may be studied. Implied values of interest rates or dividend yields may be determined from market prices of futures contracts. The worksheet has full What-if and graphics capabilities, along with a mini-simulator.

10. Hedging Dynamics (hedge.xls)
Allows the user to simulate various hedging scenarios for a particular underlying contract, and several imperfectly correlated cash, stock, and futures contracts. The program calculates the optimal hedge ratios, but allows the user to override these values, or provide a set of competing hedge portfolio weights. The program shows a price simulation and demonstrates profit and loss scenarios based on the simulations. The user can graphically determine how

well his or her hedge performed against the optimal hedge and against the underlying position. The simulation assumes that prices are generated by jointly normally distributed random proportionate changes, using historical drift and volatility and correlation parameters. The sheet uses *Crunch* to provide the four necessary data tables.

11. Options Risk Analysis (optrisk.xls)
For an underlying equity, cash, or futures position, the user can input an option position of up to 10 different exercise/maturity combinations. If the user provides prices, he can get implied volatilities using modified Black-Scholes formulae; if he provides volatilities, he gets prices. The worksheet allows the user to project an arbitrary trading scenario and shows changes in the risk parameters of the position as well as profits and losses. The user may include commissions to liquidating a position. The user can perform What-if analysis on the option variables, seeing the impact of changes in the underlying security, volatility (parallel shifts across the board), and interest rate changes. Finally, the user can graph the profit/loss scenarios. The worksheet produces three compact printouts containing all the information the user has calculated, and supplies graphical displays for analysis.

12. Margin Account Simulator (margins.xls)
This worksheet simulates the activity in a margin account for a given futures position. Simulated fluctuations in futures prices cause the balance to rise and fall; the effect of leverage is demonstrated clearly for this type of transaction. Beware of margin calls!

13. Quick European Option Pricing (quickopt.xls)
Assuming the conditions of the Black-Scholes model of option pricing, with a continuous dividend yield, this worksheet calculates option and position values for differing underlying parameters. It constructs a What-if table in Excel, and graphically demonstrates the sensitivities of option or position values with respect to the underlying parameters of the model.

Differences between *Quick European Option Pricing* and *Options Risk Analysis*
In a sense, both of these worksheet perform the same function. *Quick European Option Pricing* is intended as a beginning tool; it quickly and simply determines values, derivatives, and comparative statics in a transparent way. However, *Quick European Option Pricing* is restricted to one combination of strike price and maturity date, while *Options Risk Analysis* is not. *Options Risk Analysis* allows multiple holdings, different reporting standards, holding period returns, futures contracts, liquidating commissions, and implied volatilities. It was feared that a beginning user would get lost in the trees of *Options Risk Analysis* without seeing the forest of *Quick European Option Pricing*. *Quick European Option Pricing* solves basic option problems, *Options Risk Analysis* solves more complicated problems.

Other Programs & Files

go.exe
This program calculates the optimal holdings of the constrained portfolio in The *Super Efficient Portfolio Frontier*.

pdata.xls
This is an Excel workbook containing price information for up to 50 securities and/or indices. The *pdata.xls* workbook also provides a model for creating your own data workbooks and work sheets. Instructions for setting up and using your own data are included in this manual. The sample data can be found in the two tabs in the workbook.

DJ Data: This Dow Jones price data is used by *The Efficient Portfolio Frontier*, *The Super Efficient Portfolio Frontier*, *Index Models & Performance* and *Hedging Dynamics* for demonstration purposes. *Crunch* is connected to this sheet by default.

IBBSIN: This tab contains the Ibbotson/Sinquefield dataset of bond, bill, and equity returns along with inflation rates from 1926 to 1986.

crunch.xla
An Excel Add-In wizard program that tabulates means, standard deviations and correlations of returns for the price series provided in *pdata.xls*, or any properly formatted Excel worksheet. The results of the calculations are placed in named ranges within *Crunch*.

NMS	Names, Means, Standard Deviations, and Last Prices

CORREL	Correlation Matrix
COEFFS	Regression Coefficient
HC	NMS data on the security to be hedged
SCOEFF	Similar to NMS but with additional fields used by INDEX

Important Notes on Saving and Altering Worksheets
In general, you should not save the worksheets when you are finished computing, unless you want to keep those particular data points handy. By saving the worksheets, you may inadvertently save a change you made to the format or calculations of the worksheet. If you wish to experiment with the worksheets, we strongly encourage you to do so. However, to maintain the integrity of the original software, please save your changed files under different names than those of the original programs.

Using Crunch, a Statistical Data-Crunching Program

Crunch calculates average returns, standard deviations, and correlations from a price or return table contained in an Excel worksheet. You can use either of the default tables in *pdata.xls*, DJ Data, a database of 50 Dow Jones financial indices, or IBBSIN, the dataset of Ibbotson and Sinquefield, covering a period from 1926 to 1986, including bond, bill, and equity returns along with inflation rates. You may also create your own dataset, using the format supplied in this section.

The worksheets that use *Crunch* display two buttons on the screen for the step when *Crunch* data is needed. The **Prepare CRUNCH Data** button starts the 5 step wizard that requests the following information:

Step 1: Indicate the name and location of the Excel file with your data

Step 2: Select the worksheet with your data

Step 3: Identify the range containing your data

Step 4: Select up to ten securities to be examined, and if applicable a reference security

Step 5: Specify the type of data: price, net return, or gross return. Specify the number of data observations per year

Once these questions have been answered, *Crunch* imports the specified data and processes it to an output sheet where it is available to the worksheets that can use it.

The **Load CRUNCH Data** button transfers the data from the *Crunch* output sheet to the worksheet where you clicked the button.

Instructions for Creating Your Own Data Sheets

You can add sheets to the *pdata.xls* workbook or create a new Excel workbook. You can enter the data manually or use the Excel File|Open command to import the data from a text file, database or other worksheet. Use Excel Help if you need more information on importing data.

The data must conform to the following rules or *Crunch* may have problems processing the data and the results may not be correct:

- The data must fill a contiguous range with no blank cells.
- The top row of the data range must contain the names of the securities.
- Rows to the left and columns above the data range may contain anything; they are ignored.
- The row below the data range must be blank; the column to right of the data range must be blank.
- All data must be of the same type: price, net return, or gross return.

	IBX	COLEX	ATX	HPX	IRWIX	BLAX	INDEX
1970	130.00	65.00	25.00	37.00	25.00	88.00	61.67
1971	125.49	64.33	41.87	26.17	36.70	96.79	65.23
1972	133.36	71.29	61.24	29.81	40.80	120.40	76.15
1973	127.61	79.07	78.29	32.38	47.72	200.73	94.30

Tip: Use the left column for identifying the observation intervals (dates). Do not include the date column when the *Crunch* wizard asks you for the upper left corner of the data range. Do include the row with the security names. For example, if the cell address of IBX is *B1*, then in step 3 of the *Crunch* wizard, enter *B* in the Column text box and *1* in the Row text box. The IBX cell of the worksheet will be highlighted in yellow to confirm your selection.

The above table shows price data; the other types are net return and gross return. For example if IBM trades at 120 in one year and 132 the next, the corresponding number for each data type would be:

Price	132.00
Net Return	0.10
Gross Return	1.10

Net return equals gross return minus one. If you use gross returns or net returns the program will assume that the last price was $1. This fact proves to have little consequence except in the *Hedging Dynamics* worksheet where specific instructions help you work around it.

General Worksheet Instructions

Getting Started:
Windows 95: Click on Start. Then point to Programs|The Innovative Investor (folder)|The Innovative Investor icon and click.
Windows 3.1: Open The Innovative Investor program group. Double click the Innovative Investor icon.

Excel will be automatically launched.

The following menu screen will appear.

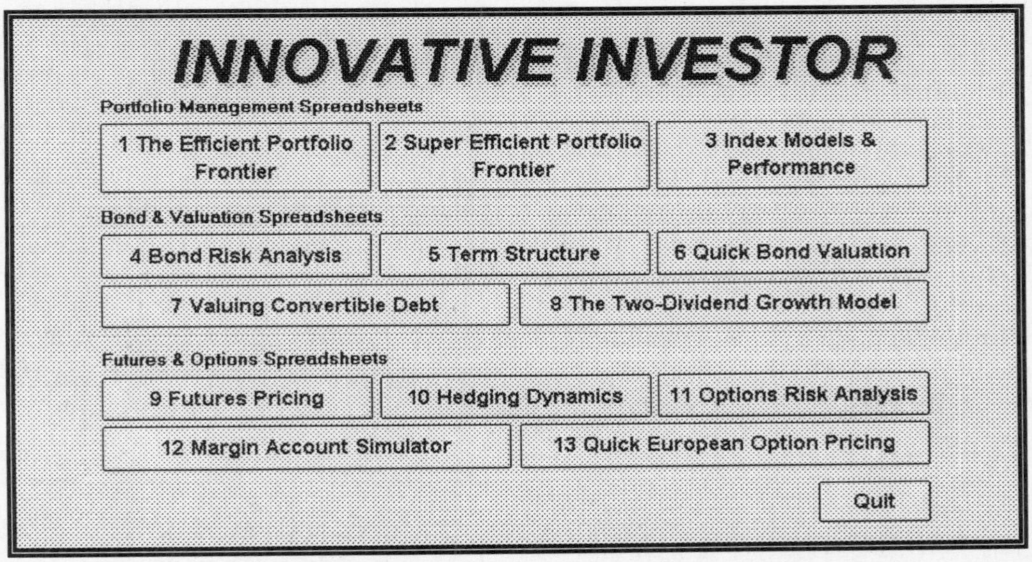
INNOVATIVE INVESTOR
Portfolio Management Spreadsheets
1 The Efficient Portfolio Frontier
2 Super Efficient Portfolio Frontier
3 Index Models & Performance
Bond & Valuation Spreadsheets
4 Bond Risk Analysis
5 Term Structure
6 Quick Bond Valuation
7 Valuing Convertible Debt
8 The Two-Dividend Growth Model
Futures & Options Spreadsheets
9 Futures Pricing
10 Hedging Dynamics
11 Options Risk Analysis
12 Margin Account Simulator
13 Quick European Option Pricing
Quit

Just click the button of the application worksheet you want.

When you click the **Quit** button of any of the application sheets you will return to this screen.

The worksheets were designed to have a consistent approach. A few conventions are common to every worksheet; they are worthwhile to learn before beginning your study.

Each sheet has a menu screen that is displayed when you open the application. You can skip to most sections of the application from the menu screen.

In most applications you will be presented a series of screens in sequence.

In the early screens you will set parameters and input data. Generally you can change anything that is displayed in blue. Most screens have a **Press Here to Continue** button that keeps you on track through each process.

If you need to back up you can always return to the application menu by pressing the **Menu** button that appears on almost every screen. Then click the button that takes you to the screen you want. In some screens you can use the Page-Down, Page-Up, Tab, and Shift-Tab keys as navigational shortcuts.

For the most part, cell ranges and formulas have been protected making it difficult for you to inadvertently change a protected cell's contents. You may remove protection if you wish. Do so at your own risk.

Normally you will not need to save your worksheets. If you need to save an application do so with the menu command File|SaveAs and give the file a new name. Otherwise you may overwrite the original worksheets with modifications that do not perform as intended. If this happens restore the original application *.*xls* file from your installation disk.

The following pages contain examples of output and clarifying discussion where needed. You can use the introductory examples contained in each sheet to match the printed examples in this manual and verify the integrity of each worksheet.

Worksheet 1
The Efficient Portfolio Frontier
Specific Instructions and a Numerical Example

EFFPORT.XLS

Following are output and commentary to accompany the first worksheet, *The Efficient Portfolio Frontier*.

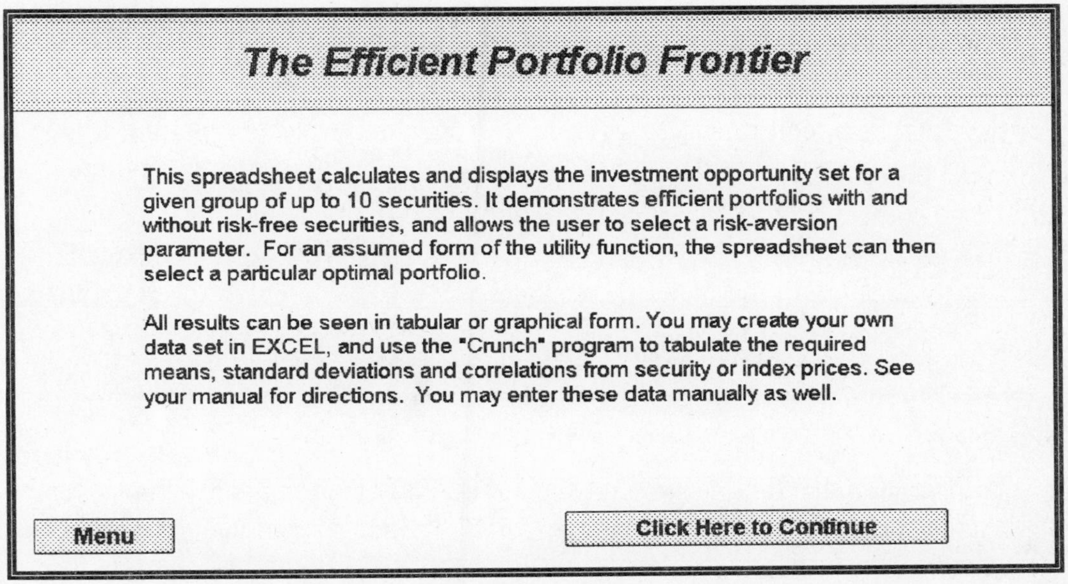
The Efficient Portfolio Frontier
This spreadsheet calculates and displays the investment opportunity set for a given group of up to 10 securities. It demonstrates efficient portfolios with and without risk-free securities, and allows the user to select a risk-aversion parameter. For an assumed form of the utility function, the spreadsheet can then select a particular optimal portfolio.
All results can be seen in tabular or graphical form. You may create your own data set in EXCEL, and use the "Crunch" program to tabulate the required means, standard deviations and correlations from security or index prices. See your manual for directions. You may enter these data manually as well.
Menu
Click Here to Continue

Steps 1 and 2 are self-explanatory. The user can provide data by typing them in manually, or by using the *Crunch* utility to process periodic data stored in an Excel spreadsheet. *Crunch* adjusts for the format of the data and the data frequency. Note under the correlation matrix that you can quickly copy a formula or value into the correlation matrix. Usually this step won't be required, but it may save you from typing a lot of zeroes into the correlation cells, for example. Riskless assets ($\sigma = 0$) may not be introduced at this point; you may introduce one later.

Step 1. Please provide the names, expected return and standard deviations of up to 10 securities (figures in decimals).

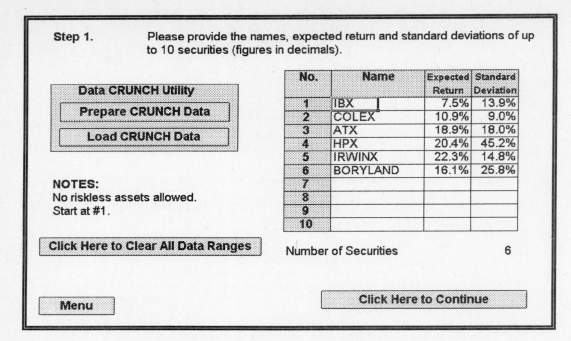

Data CRUNCH Utility

[Prepare CRUNCH Data]

[Load CRUNCH Data]

No.	Name	Expected Return	Standard Deviation
1	IBX	7.5%	13.9%
2	COLEX	10.9%	9.0%
3	ATX	18.9%	18.0%
4	HPX	20.4%	45.2%
5	IRWINX	22.3%	14.8%
6	BORYLAND	16.1%	25.8%
7			
8			
9			
10			

NOTES:
No riskless assets allowed.
Start at #1.

[Click Here to Clear All Data Ranges]

Number of Securities 6

[Menu] [Click Here to Continue]

Step 2. Fill in the correlation matrix only through column 6.

	Correlations >>	2	3	4	5	6	7	8	9	10
		COLEX		HPX		BORYLAND		0		0
No.	Name		ATX		IRWINX		0		0	
1	IBX	0.00	-0.21	0.13	0.39	-0.15	0.00	0.00	0.00	0.00
2	COLEX	1.00	-0.05	0.54	-0.09	-0.42	0.00	0.00	0.00	0.00
3	ATX	......	1.00	-0.01	0.45	-0.11	0.00	0.00	0.00	0.00
4	HPX	......	......	1.00	0.03	-0.16	0.00	0.00	0.00	0.00
5	IRWINX	......	......	......	1.00	-0.16	0.00	0.00	0.00	0.00
6	BORYLAND	......	......	......	......	1.00	0.00	0.00	0.00	0.00
7	0	......	......	......	......	......	1.00	0.00	0.00	0.00
8	0	......	......	......	......	......	......	1.00	0.00	0.00
9	0	......	......	......	......	......	......	......	1.00	0.00
10	0	......	......	......	......	......	......	......	......	1.00

Optional: [Click Here to Copy this Formula or Value into Matrix >>>] 0.00

[Menu] [Click Here to Continue]

Whenever you change anything before step 3 (returns and correlations), you must click the **Click Here to Recalculate** button on the *Step 3* screen. Changes after step 3 do not affect the calculation of the efficient frontier for risky assets. They do not need to be recalculated when we change characteristics of the riskless assets or the utility functions.

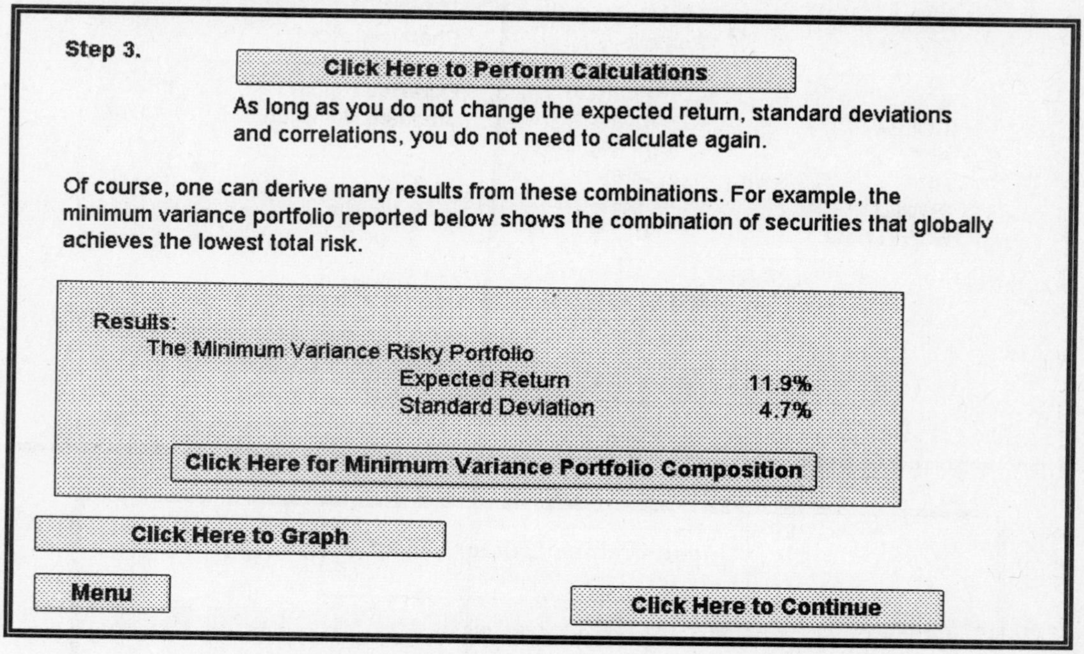
Step 3.
Click Here to Perform Calculations
As long as you do not change the expected return, standard deviations and correlations, you do not need to calculate again.
Of course, one can derive many results from these combinations. For example, the minimum variance portfolio reported below shows the combination of securities that globally achieves the lowest total risk.
Results:
The Minimum Variance Risky Portfolio
Expected Return 11.9%
Standard Deviation 4.7%
Click Here for Minimum Variance Portfolio Composition
Click Here to Graph
Menu
Click Here to Continue

The **Click Here for Minimum Variance Portfolio Composition** button will display the exact combination of risky assets that achieve the minimum variance.

The **Click Here to Graph** button displays the information in visual form. These two screens appear on the next page.

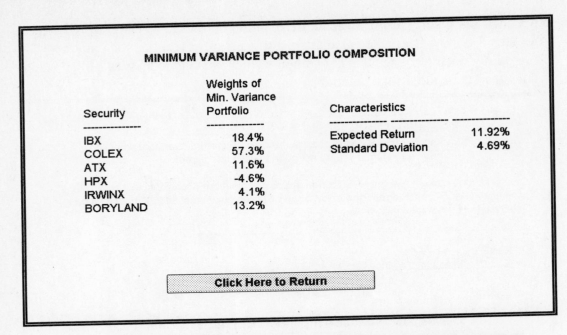

MINIMUM VARIANCE PORTFOLIO COMPOSITION

Security	Weights of Min. Variance Portfolio
IBX	18.4%
COLEX	57.3%
ATX	11.6%
HPX	-4.6%
IRWINX	4.1%
BORYLAND	13.2%

Characteristics	
Expected Return	11.92%
Standard Deviation	4.69%

Click Here to Return

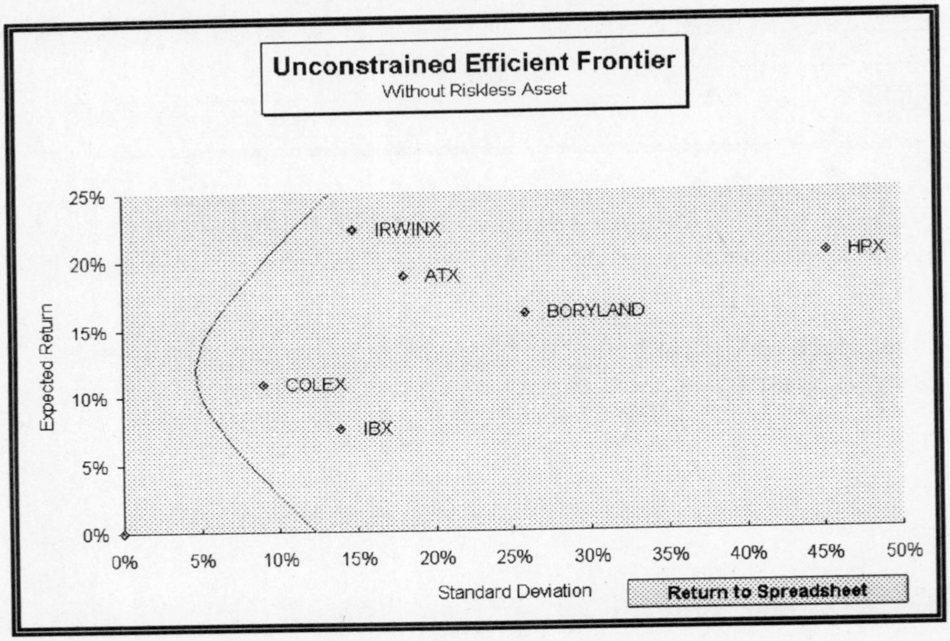
Unconstrained Efficient Frontier
Without Riskless Asset
Expected Return
25%
20%
15%
10%
5%
0%
IRWINX
HPX
ATX
BORYLAND
COLEX
IBX
0%
5%
10%
15%
20%
25%
30%
35%
40%
45%
50%
Standard Deviation
Return to Spreadsheet

Step 4. Choose a target rate of return to find the risk level & portfolio composition to best achieve that return.

On the graph, this operation corresponds to selecting the portfolio with the lowest total risk for a given expected return. The portfolio composition indicates how one could attain that combination of risk and return.

For this example, if you choose an expected return below 11.9%, your portfolio would lie on the inefficient segment of the portfolio frontier.

Target Return Portfolio

Desired Expected Return	25.0%
Standard Deviation	13.3%

Click Here for Portfolio Composition

Click Here to Graph

Menu

Click Here to Continue

Once again we can see the portfolio weights that achieve the target return most efficiently with risky assets only. You indicate the desired expected return, and the computer will show the efficient portfolio weights. Q: What happens when you have a desired expected return target that is too low?

PORTFOLIO COMPOSITIONS

Security	Weights of Min. Variance Portfolio	Weights of Target Portfolio	Target Return
IBX	18.4%	-55.5%	25.0%
COLEX	57.3%	38.3%	
ATX	11.6%	-8.8%	Standard
HPX	-4.6%	5.1%	Deviation
IRWINX	4.1%	99.2%	--------------
BORYLAND	13.2%	21.7%	13.3%

Now you may introduce a riskless security to the analysis. Be sure to note its effects on portfolio composition. In particular, the presence of the riskless asset generates a unique tangency portfolio.

Step 5. If a riskless security exists, enter its return here. The spreadsheet determines the corresponding market portfolio, and the highest possible CAL. See Bodie, Kane and Marcus Chapter 7 for an explanation.

Is there a riskfree security? (1-YES,2-NO)		1
Riskfree Rate of Return (Choose a riskless rate of return below 11.9%)		5.0%
Characteristics of Tangency Portfolio	Expected Return	15.4%
	Standard Deviation	5.8%
	Reward/Variability	1.81

Click Here for Tangency Portfolio Composition

Click Here to Graph

Menu

Click Here to Continue

The composition of the tangency portfolio appears below.

TANGENCY PORTFOLIO COMPOSITION

Security	Weights of Tangency Portfolio	Characteristics of Tangency Portfolio	
IBX	-1.3%	Mean	15.4%
COLEX	52.2%	Std Dev	5.8%
ATX	6.2%	Reward/Variability	1.81
HPX	-2.0%		
IRWINX	29.5%	Risk-free rate	5.00%
BORYLAND	15.5%		

This is the corresponding graphical output:

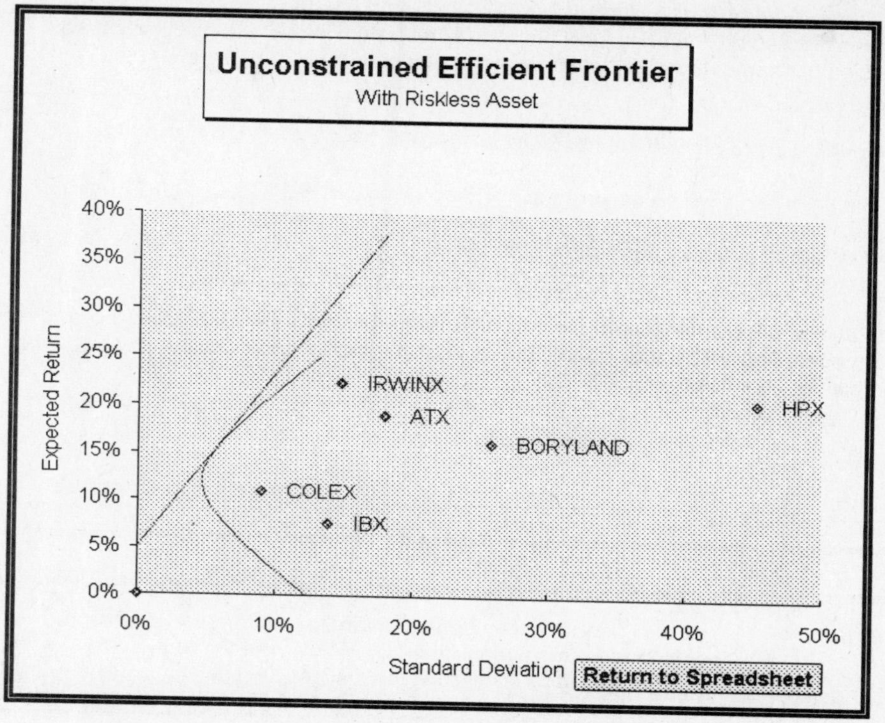
Unconstrained Efficient Frontier
With Riskless Asset
40%
35%
30%
25%
20%
15%
10%
5%
0%
Expected Return
IRWINX
ATX
HPX
BORYLAND
COLEX
IBX
0%
10%
20%
30%
40%
50%
Standard Deviation
Return to Spreadsheet

Up to this point, we have made no assumptions regarding the portfolio manager's level of risk aversion. We introduce a particular utility function, and examine optimal portfolio choice in the presence or the absence of a riskless security.

Step 6. Selecting the optimal portfolio from the set of efficient portfolios.

For this discussion, the utility function is expected return minus one-half times a risk aversion parameter times the variance of the portfolio.

Do you want to graph the utility function? (1-YES,2-NO) 1

The utility curve will be centered at standard deviation 18.1%.
You may choose how far to show the utility function in each direction by putting a decimal number here: 0.0% (Zero for default)

Your choice of an optimal portfolio may differ from other investors' choices. To study these differences, you will be allowed to choose a risk parameter and calculate an optimal portfolio for your risk aversion level.

Menu **Click Here to Continue**

Step 7. You may now select an optimal portfolio from the set of efficient portfolios. Enter your risk aversion below; use PgUp twice to see the effect of adding or eliminating the riskless security.

Case I: With Riskless Asset		Case II: No Riskless Asset	
Risk parameter (A):	10	Risk parameter (A):	10
Optimal Expected Return:	37.8%	Optimal Expected Return:	22.9%
Standard Deviation:	18.1%	Standard Deviation:	11.5%
Utility:	0.21	Utility:	0.16
Wts: Market Portfolio:	3.15		
Riskfree Asset:	-2.15		

Net Portfolio Weights **Click Here for Optimal Portfolio Composition**

Click Here to Graph

Menu **Click Here to Continue**

The optimal portfolio weights follow:

OPTIMAL PORTFOLIO COMPOSITIONS

Security	Weights with Riskless Asset	Weights without Riskless Asset
IBX	-4.2%	-43.8%
COLEX	164.4%	41.3%
ATX	19.4%	-5.6%
HPX	-6.4%	3.5%
IRWINX	93.0%	84.1%
BORYLAND	48.7%	20.4%

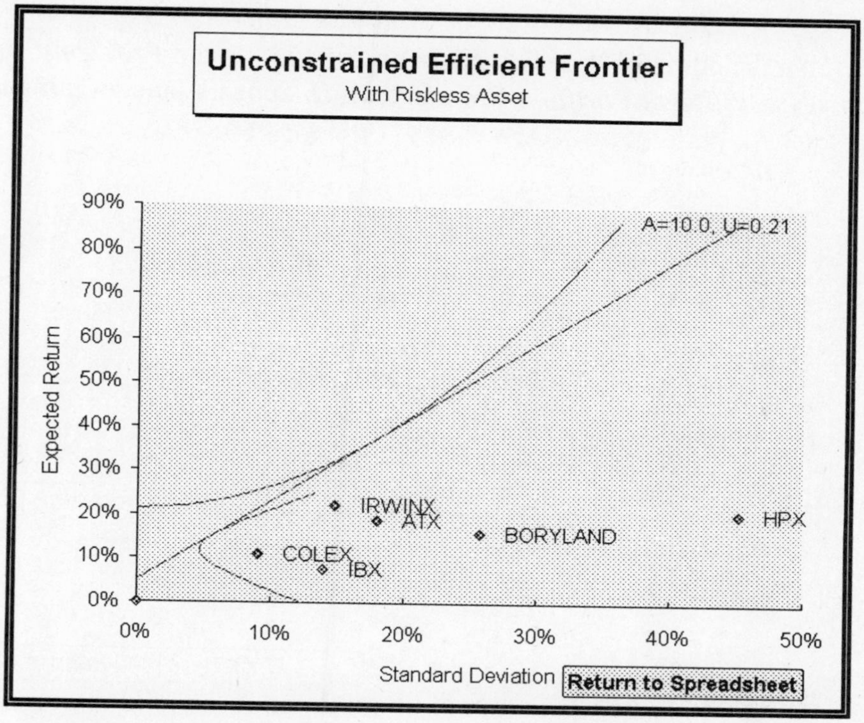
Unconstrained Efficient Frontier
With Riskless Asset
Expected Return
90%
80%
70%
60%
50%
40%
30%
20%
10%
0%
A=10.0, U=0.21
IRWINX
ATX
BORYLAND
HPX
COLEX
IBX
0%
10%
20%
30%
40%
50%
Standard Deviation
Return to Spreadsheet

Every attempt was made to make the graphs look aesthetically pleasing. However, for your particular presentation, the steps or axis limits may look wrong to your eye. You can change all these values in this last page of the worksheet.

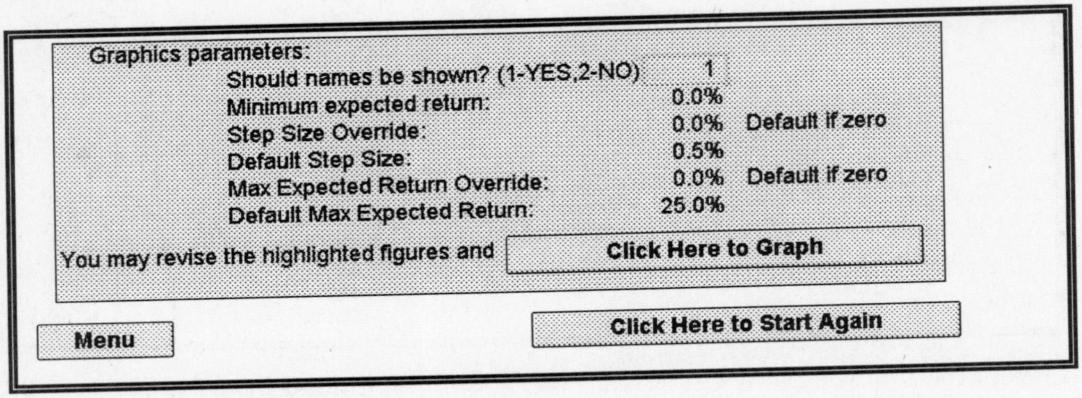
Graphics parameters:
Should names be shown? (1-YES,2-NO)
1
Minimum expected return:
0.0%
Step Size Override:
0.0%
Default if zero
Default Step Size:
0.5%
Max Expected Return Override:
0.0%
Default if zero
Default Max Expected Return:
25.0%
You may revise the highlighted figures and
Click Here to Graph
Menu
Click Here to Start Again

Test your understanding of this worksheet by completing the *Problems to Accompany The Efficient Portfolio Frontier*, which appears later in this manual.

Worksheet 2
The Super Efficient Portfolio Frontier
Specific Instructions and a Numerical Example

SUPEREFF.XLS

The structure of the *The Super Efficient Portfolio Frontier* worksheet is very similar to that of *The Efficient Portfolio Frontier*. The inputs are the same, including the expected returns, standard deviations and correlations between securities. However, *The Efficient Portfolio Frontier* computes the optimal security holdings assuming short sales are allowed; in real-world investing, it may be too costly or impossible to short sell certain assets. In addition, institutional requirements often place restrictions on the feasible asset allocations. For example, a pension fund may be required to have at least 80% of its holdings in stocks and bonds. This worksheet answers the question, "What are my optimal portfolio holdings when I am faced with constraints on my investment policy?"

The menu options are listed below.

Intro: Worksheet introduction

Data Section:

Returns: Input expected returns and standard deviations

Correlations: Input correlation matrix

Calcs Section:

Calculations: Calculate unconstrained portfolio optima (must be recalculated any time returns, standard deviations, or correlations are changed)

Target: Finds holdings for efficient risky portfolio given a target return level

Riskless: Finds holdings in tangency portfolio

Utility: Sets utility specifications

Optimal: Finds optimal holdings for given level of risk aversion

Graph: Graph the efficient portfolio set

Restricted: Input constraints on allowable investments

Print: Print selected ranges

Quit: Return to Innovative Investor menu

The **Intro** button on the *Menu* screen displays the following screen:

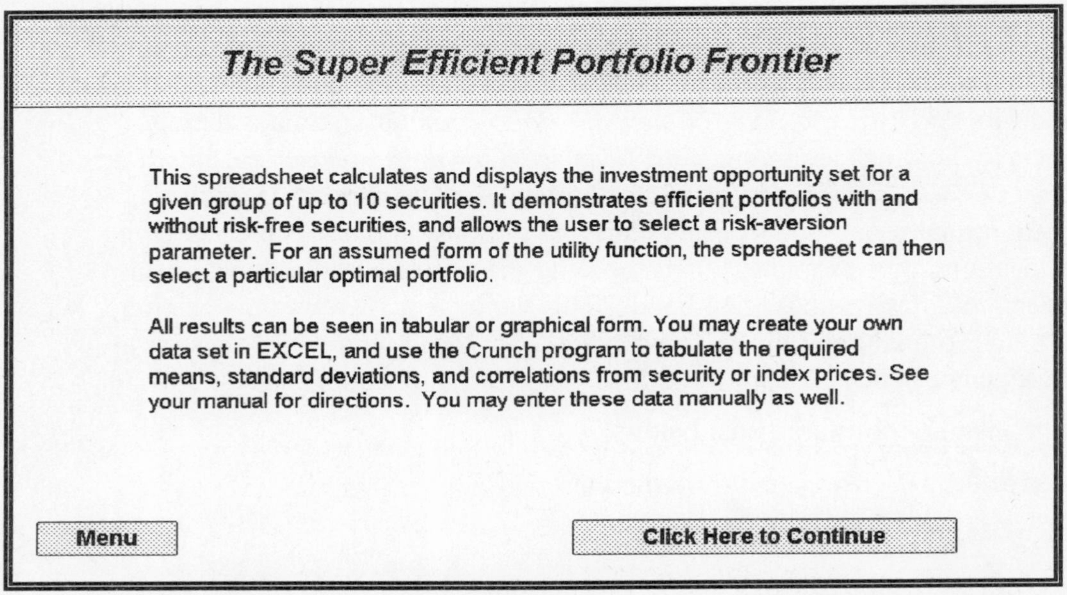
The Super Efficient Portfolio Frontier
This spreadsheet calculates and displays the investment opportunity set for a given group of up to 10 securities. It demonstrates efficient portfolios with and without risk-free securities, and allows the user to select a risk-aversion parameter. For an assumed form of the utility function, the spreadsheet can then select a particular optimal portfolio.
All results can be seen in tabular or graphical form. You may create your own data set in EXCEL, and use the Crunch program to tabulate the required means, standard deviations, and correlations from security or index prices. See your manual for directions. You may enter these data manually as well.
Menu
Click Here to Continue

The **Click Here to Continue** button displays the first of seven steps. The first step is to provide the appropriate statistical data. If historical data are used, the *Crunch* program can be used to process the data in Excel files for use by *The Super Efficient Portfolio Frontier*. Use the **Prepare CRUNCH Data** button to calculate the expected return, standard deviation, and correlation figures required for steps one and two. Click the **Load CRUNCH Data** to move the data into the *The Super Efficient Portfolio Frontier* forms. Help screens in *Crunch* explain how to configure historical data for import. You can enter the data manually by using the **Click Here to Clear All Data Ranges**, then type in the data in the two screens shown on the next page.

Step 1. Please provide the names, expected return, and standard deviations of up to 10 securities (figures in decimals).

Data CRUNCH Utilities

Prepare CRUNCH Data

Import CRUNCH Data

No.	Name	Expected Return	Standard Deviation
1	Stocks	12.1%	21.0%
2	Bonds	8.0%	13.5%
3	Real Estate	3.5%	3.3%
4	Commodities	4.5%	15.0%
5			
6			
7			
8			
9			
10			

NOTES:
No riskless assets allowed.
Start at #1.

Click Here to Clear All Data Ranges

Number of Securities 4

Menu

Click Here to Continue

Use the **Click Here to Continue** button to display the correlation matrix.

Step 2. Fill in the correlation matrix only through column 4.

Correlations >>		2 Bonds	3 Real Estate	4 Commodities	5	6	7	8	9	10
No.	Name									
1	Stocks	0.10	-0.07	-0.02	0.00	0.00	0.00	0.00	0.00	0.00
2	Bonds	1.00	0.22	-0.17	0.00	0.00	0.00	0.00	0.00	0.00
3	Real Estate	......	1.00	0.41	0.00	0.00	0.00	0.00	0.00	0.00
4	Commodities	......	......	1.00	0.00	0.00	0.00	0.00	0.00	0.00
5		......	......	......	1.00	0.00	0.00	0.00	0.00	0.00
6		......	......	......	......	1.00	0.00	0.00	0.00	0.00
7		......	......	......	......	......	1.00	0.00	0.00	0.00
8		......	......	......	......	......	......	1.00	0.00	0.00
9		......	......	......	......	......	......	......	1.00	0.00
10		......	......	......	......	......	......	......	......	1.00

Optional: Click Here to Copy this Formula or Value into Matrix >>> 0.00

Menu

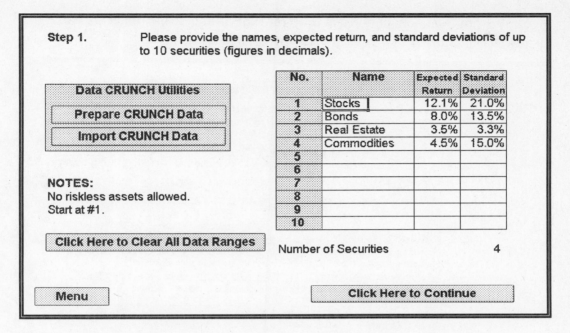

Click Here to Continue

If you want to use a single correlation figure for all the assets, enter its value in the lower right corner and click the button to its left.

Step 3. [Click Here to Perform Calculations]

As long as you do not change the expected return, standard deviations and correlations, you do not need to calculate again.

Of course, one can derive many results from these combinations. For example, the minimum variance portfolio reported below shows the combination of securities that globally achieves the lowest total risk.

Results:
The Minimum Variance Risky Portfolio

Expected Return	3.7%
Standard Deviation	3.2%

[Click Here for Minimum Variance Portfolio Composition]

[Click Here to Graph]

[Menu] [Click Here to Continue]

Use the **Click Here to Recalculate** button to perform the unconstrained calculations. The characteristics of the minimum variance portfolio are calculated at the same time. Use **Click Here for Minimum Variance Portfolio Composition** to display the following screen

MINIMUM VARIANCE PORTFOLIO COMPOSITION

Security	Weights of Min. Variance Portfolio	Characteristics	
Stocks	3.5%	Expected return	3.7%
Bonds	-1.6%	Std deviation	3.2%
Real Estate	103.2%		
Commodities	-5.1%		

In step 4 you may choose any expected return and learn how to achieve that expected return most efficiently from a portfolio of risky assets:

Step 4. Choose a target rate of return to find the risk level & portfolio composition to best achieve that return.

On the graph, this operation corresponds to selecting the portfolio with the lowest total risk for a given expected return. The portfolio composition indicates how one could attain that combination of risk and return.

For this example, if you choose an expected return below 3.7%, your portfolio would lie on the inefficient segment of the portfolio frontier.

Target Return Portfolio

Desired Expected Return	17.0%
Standard Deviation	25.5%

Click Here for Portfolio Composition

Click Here to Graph

Menu

Click Here to Continue

Click Here for Portfolio Composition provides the following details.

PORTFOLIO COMPOSITION

Security	Minimum Variance	Target
Stocks	3.5%	84.1%
Bonds	-1.6%	126.3%
Real Estate	103.2%	-169.0%
Commodities	-5.1%	58.6%

Characteristics	
Expected return	17.0%
Std deviation	25.5%

By adding a risk-free asset in step 5, we can find the tangency portfolio:

Step 5. Enter the risk-free return here. The spreadsheet determines the corresponding market portfolio, and the highest possible CAL. See Bodie, Kane and Marcus Chapter 7 for an explanation.

Riskfree Rate of Return 3.0%
(Choose a riskless rate of return below 3.7%)

Characteristics of Tangency Portfolio	Expected Return	7.8%
	Standard Deviation	8.5%
	Reward/Variability	0.57

Click Here for Tangency Portfolio Composition

Click Here to Graph

Menu **Click Here to Continue**

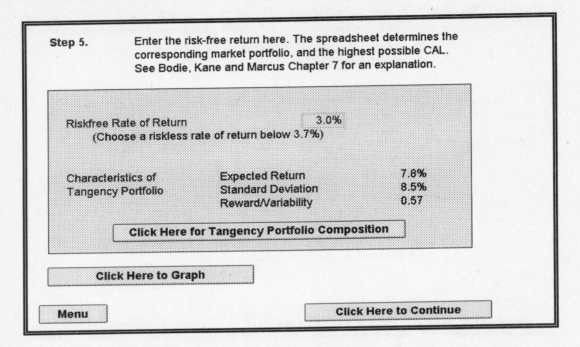

Use **Click Here for Tangency Portfolio Composition** to see the composition details.

TANGENCY PORTFOLIO COMPOSITION

Security	Weights of Tangency Portfolio	Characteristics of Tangency Portfolio	
Stocks	28.7%	Mean	7.8%
Bonds	38.4%	Std Dev	8.5%
Real Estate	18.1%	Reward/Variability	0.57
Commodities	14.8%		
		Risk-free rate	3.0%

We add utility considerations in step 6.

Step 6. Selecting the optimal portfolio from the set of efficient portfolios. (UNCONSTRAINED)

For this discussion, the utility function is expected return minus one-half times a risk aversion parameter times the variance of the portfolio.

Do you want to graph the utility function? (1-YES,2-NO): 2

The utility curve will be centered at standard deviation 0.0%.
You may choose how far to show the utility function in each direction by putting a decimal number here: 0.0% (Zero for default)

Your choice of an optimal portfolio may differ from other investors' choices. To study these differences, you will be allowed to choose a risk parameter and calculate an optimal portfolio for your risk aversion level.

Menu

Click Here to Continue

Enter the risk-aversion coefficient in step 7.

Step 7. You may now select an optimal portfolio from the set of efficient portfolios. Enter your risk aversion below; Click Here to see the effect of adding or eliminating the riskless security.

With Riskless Asset

Risk parameter (A):	5
Optimal Expected Return:	9.5%
Standard Deviation:	11.4%
Utility:	0.06
Wts: Market Portfolio:	1.33
Riskfree Asset:	-0.33

Click Here for Optimal Portfolio Composition

Click Here to Graph

Menu

Click Here to Continue

Click Here for Optimal Portfolio Composition shows the unconstrained holdings. **Click Here to Graph** for the diagram of the efficient frontier.

OPTIMAL PORTFOLIO COMPOSITIONS

Security	Weights with Riskless Asset
Stocks	38.3%
Bonds	51.3%
Real Estate	24.1%
Commodities	19.8%

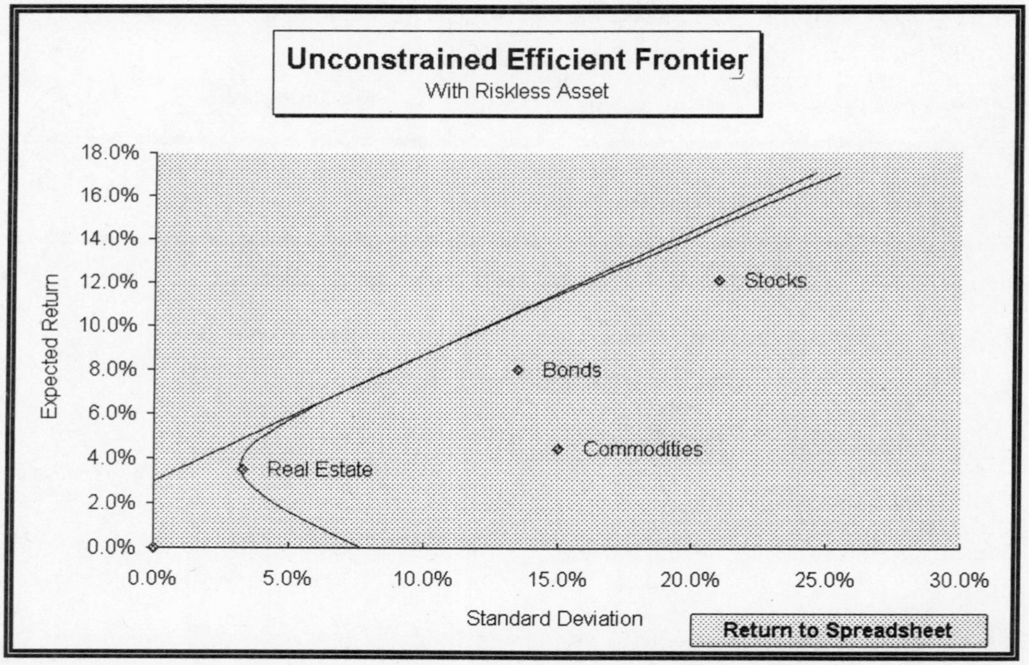
Unconstrained Efficient Frontier
With Riskless Asset
18.0%
16.0%
14.0%
12.0%
10.0%
8.0%
6.0%
4.0%
2.0%
0.0%
Expected Return
Stocks
Bonds
Commodities
Real Estate
0.0%
5.0%
10.0%
15.0%
20.0%
25.0%
30.0%
Standard Deviation
Return to Spreadsheet

At this point, *The Super Efficient Portfolio Frontier* makes a departure from the capabilities of *The Efficient Portfolio Frontier*. In the next screen, we may enter any linear constraints that might affect our asset allocation. For example, suppose we must satisfy the following restrictions:

Stocks must comprise at least 50% of our portfolio.

Bonds must comprise no more than 40% of our portfolio.

We may not borrow or lend.

The worksheet automatically assumes that short-selling is not possible; all weights must be positive. If you would like to know the optimal allocation with no short-selling, use the **Click Here to Erase Constraints** to clear the constraint range and continue.

You may enter up to eight additional constraints. The worksheet accepts only greater than (>) constraints or equals (=) constraints. The first constraint implies that

$1w_s >= 0.50$

where w_s is the proportion of our portfolio allotted to stocks. In the matrix below, this is entered as

$1w_s + 0w_b + 0w_r + 0w_c > 0.50$

The program knows that we really mean "greater than or equal to." All non-zero coefficients must be typed in the appropriate spot in the matrix. Also, the sign (>) must appear under the SIGNS heading.

The second constraint states that $w_b <= 0.40$. This must be converted to a (>) constraint to be accepted by the worksheet. Remember that if you multiply an inequality by (-1), the inequality changes sign. Therefore we have

$0w_s - 1w_b + 0w_r + 0w_c > -0.40$

For the last constraint, we require that there be no borrowing or lending. This can be accomplished by requiring that the sum of the risky allocations be 1.00.

This is accomplished by the following constraint:

$$1w_s + 1w_b + 1w_r + 1w_c = 1.00$$

In the worksheet, the entries look like this:

Constrained Asset Allocation

Current unconstrained allocation:
38% 51% 24% 20% 0% 0% 0% 0% 0% 0%

Risk-free allocation: -33%

Click Here to Erase Constraints

Enter constraints below: (Positivity constraints are automatic)

Stocks	Bonds	Real Estate	Commodities						SIGNS	
1									>	0.50
	-1								>	-0.40
1	1	1	1						=	1.00

Menu | Enter > or = constraints | Click Here for Optimal Asset Allocations

The **Click Here for Optimal Asset** button displays both the unconstrained optimum and the constrained optimum side by side. The lower right corner indicates the change in expected return, volatility, and utility due to the constraints.

Optimal Asset Allocations

Asset	Unconstrained	Constrained		(For your reference) Prior Constrained	
Stocks	38.26%	50.00%		50.00%	
Bonds	51.26%	38.43%		38.42%	
Real Estate	24.12%	0.00%		0.00%	
Commodities	19.79%	11.57%		11.58%	
	0.00%				
	0.00%				
	0.00%				
	0.00%				
	0.00%				
	0.00%				
Risk-free	-33.43%	0.00%	Changes	0.00%	Changes
Expected return	9.46%	9.64%	0.18%	9.64%	0.18%
Volatility	11.37%	19.32%	7.95%	19.35%	7.99%
Utility (CEQ HPR)	6.23%	0.32%	-5.91%	0.28%	-5.95%

Menu

Click Here to Continue

Test your understanding of *this worksheet* by completing the *Problems to Accompany The Super Efficient Portfolio Frontier*, which appear later in this manual.

Worksheet 3
Index Models and Performance
Specific Instructions and a Numerical Example

INDEX.XLS

This worksheet shows the relationship between the expected return on as many as 10 securities and the security market line. The basic calculations are identical to those found in a beta-book. However, the user has the flexibility to change assumptions about the risk-free interest rate and the average return premium to learn how these assumptions affect the relationship between security returns and the security market line.

The worksheet can also be used to conduct performance measurement under a single-index model. Four measurement techniques are used: those of Sharpe, Treynor, Jensen (alpha), and the Appraisal ratio.

The *Crunch* program formats historic data for use in the *Index Models and Performance* worksheet. You can run it from within the worksheet. You may use your own data or some of the data included with *The Innovative Investor*. Refer to the *Using Crunch* chapter in this manual for more details.

Here are the Menu buttons available with this worksheet:

Intro: Displays the worksheet introduction

Load: Loads *Crunch* historical data

Beta: Shows beta-book calculations

SML: Plots the security market line

Performance: Calculates performance measurements.

Rank: Ranks securities using four performance measurements.

Print: Prints your results.

Quit: Leave the *Index Models and Performance* worksheet.

Here is the text of the introductory screen:

Index Models and Performance

This program depends on the historical data you provide. Use Crunch from the next screen to prepare and load your data. Based on the historical data, this template plots a security market line, and shows the relationship of several assets or portfolios to the security market line. This can be interpreted as a CAPM spreadsheet if the benchmark to the portfolio is the market portfolio, and the CAPM assumptions are true. In general, however, it is better to think of this model as a single-index measurement model.

This spreadsheet can also be used to measure portfolio performance. The performance of up to 10 assets can be compared to a benchmark portfolio. You may use the data provided in the package, or follow the instructions in the Crunch documentation to use your own data files.

Menu | Click Here to Continue

Crunch stores the data from its last use. You can use this data by clicking the **Load Crunch Data** button or you can format different data by clicking the **Prepare Crunch Data** button. Then click the **Load** button.

For the sample calculation, we used the Dow Jones data file (pdata.xls) and selected VWCRSP, the value-weighted CRSP index, as the benchmark. Then, we chose the first 10 securities available, skipping the EWCRSP index.

BETA-BOOK DATA

BENCHMARK	Last	Ret	Std Dev		Observations:	300
VWCRSP	#N/A	9.41%	14.81%		Frequency/yr:	12

INDIVIDUAL SECURITIES/PORTFOLIOS

#	Tkr	Last	Beta	Alpha	R-Sqr	Resid Std Dev	Sb	Sa	Adj Beta
1	T	#N/A	0.549	0.004	29.36%	0.0365	0.049	0.002	0.699
2	BS	#N/A	1.155	-0.005	37.91%	0.0633	0.086	0.004	1.103
3	BA	#N/A	1.358	0.007	28.54%	0.0920	0.124	0.005	1.239
4	CHU	#N/A	0.926	0.003	33.10%	0.0564	0.076	0.003	0.950
5	KO	#N/A	0.892	0.005	39.65%	0.0471	0.064	0.003	0.928
6	DD	#N/A	0.890	-0.002	39.68%	0.0470	0.064	0.003	0.927
7	EK	#N/A	0.860	0.001	35.60%	0.0495	0.067	0.003	0.907
8	XON	#N/A	0.710	0.005	35.98%	0.0406	0.055	0.002	0.807
9	GE	#N/A	1.059	-0.001	51.03%	0.0444	0.060	0.003	1.039
10	GM	#N/A	0.818	0.002	36.41%	0.0463	0.063	0.003	0.878

Menu | **Prepare CRUNCH Data** | **Load CRUNCH Data** | **Click Here to Continue**

If you use the **Load** button on the *Menu* screen, you will be transported to the *Beta-Book Data* screen automatically.

In the *Beta-Book Data* screen, data are reported using the frequency you specified in the data; for example, the alpha applies to the monthly alpha for the securities in this case since the data was recorded monthly.

The calculation of the security market line depends on the assumptions you enter on this screen. Under the CAPM, for example, if the market is correct on average, the average excess return should be zero. We assumed in this case that the average excess return for this sample is 2%. We allow you to vary this assumption to see how the implied risk-free rate changes. Alternatively, you may simply overwrite the risk-free rate to get a revised security market line.

SECURITY MARKET LINE DETERMINATION

We determine the risk-free rate by assuming the average excess return is zero across the securities you included in your analysis. If you change the average alpha by over-writing it, the risk-free rate will be adjusted accordingly. You may over-write any of the three values below.

Keep over-write values to zero to use the defaults.

To see the graph after any change you make.

[Click Here to Graph]

	Default	Over-write	Use
Average excess return	0.00%	2.00%	2.00%
Risk-free rate	4.00%	0.00%	4.00%
Market rate	9.41%	0.00%	9.41%

[Click Here to Continue]

[Menu]

After you change the SML assumptions, you may graph the implied security market line by using the **Click Here to Graph** button.

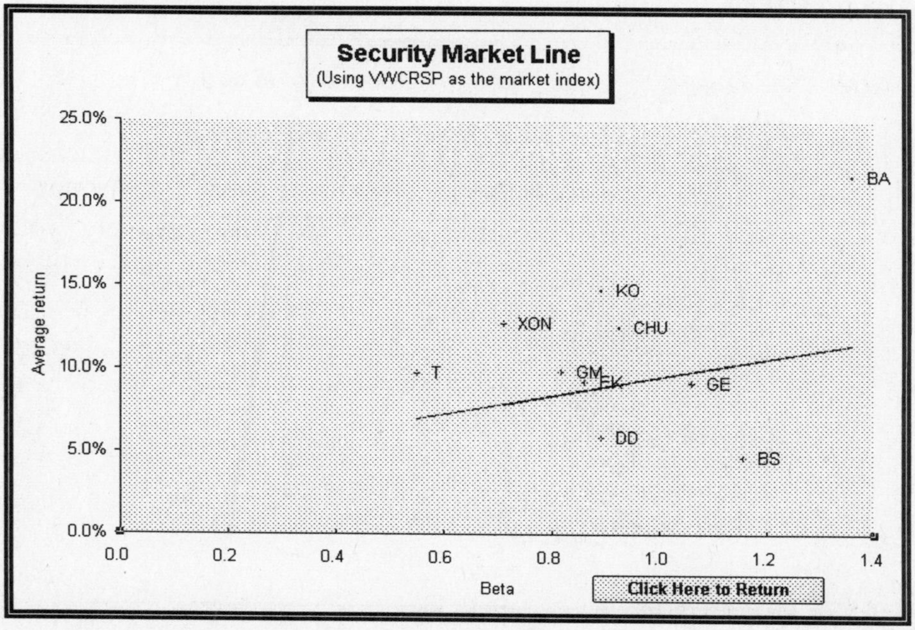

Security Market Line
(Using VWCRSP as the market index)
Average return
25.0%
20.0%
15.0%
10.0%
5.0%
0.0%
0.0
0.2
0.4
0.6
0.8
1.0
1.2
1.4
Beta
BA
KO
XON
CHU
T
GM
EK
GE
DD
BS
Click Here to Return

SUMMARY of PERFORMANCE MEASURES Raw Scores

This section is relevant if you want to measure the performance of assets or funds relative to your benchmark portfolio.

Tkr	Return	StdDev	SML	Sharpe	Treynor	Alpha	Appraisal
T	9.70%	15.00%	6.97%	0.38	0.10	0.03	0.75
BS	4.67%	27.79%	10.25%	0.02	0.01	-0.06	-0.88
BA	21.64%	37.65%	11.35%	0.47	0.13	0.10	1.12
CHU	12.49%	23.83%	9.01%	0.36	0.09	0.03	0.62
KO	14.74%	20.98%	8.83%	0.51	0.12	0.06	1.26
DD	5.89%	20.93%	8.82%	0.09	0.02	-0.03	-0.62
EK	9.18%	21.35%	8.65%	0.24	0.06	0.01	0.11
XON	12.72%	17.54%	7.84%	0.50	0.12	0.05	1.20
GE	9.07%	21.96%	9.73%	0.23	0.05	-0.01	-0.15
GM	9.77%	20.07%	8.42%	0.29	0.07	0.01	0.29

Click Here to Continue

Menu

For performance measurement purposes, we may think of each of the securities as an individual fund managed by an investment manager. Who performed best of the managers? Four performance measurements are calculated and ranked in this evaluation screen.

PERFORMANCE MEASURES **RANK STATISTICS**

This table ranks the securities or portfolios within each of the four rating systems.

Tkr	Sharpe	Treynor	Alpha	Appraisal
T	4	4	5	4
BS	10	10	10	10
BA	3	1	1	3
CHU	5	5	4	5
KO	1	3	2	1
DD	9	9	9	9
EK	7	7	7	7
XON	2	2	3	2
GE	8	8	8	8
GM	6	6	6	6

Click Here to Sort (if necessary)

Click Here to Graph

Click Here to Restart

Menu

You can retabulate the ranks by clicking the **Click Here to Sort** button. In some cases, the ranks may differ. This is conveniently summarized by the graph below.

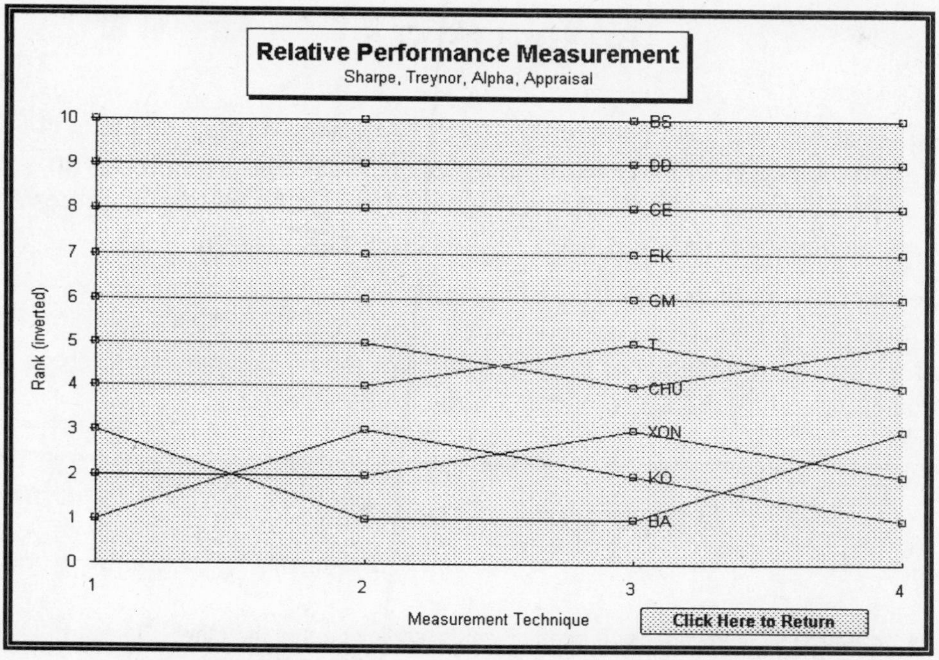
Relative Performance Measurement
Sharpe, Treynor, Alpha, Appraisal
Rank (inverted)
10
9
8
7
6
5
4
3
2
1
0
BS
DD
CE
EK
GM
T
CHU
XON
KO
BA
1
2
3
4
Measurement Technique
Click Here to Return

Test your understanding of this worksheet by completing the *Problems to Accompany Index Models and Performance*, which appears later in this manual.

Worksheet 4
Bond Risk Analysis
Specific Instructions and a Numerical Example

BONDRISK.XLS

This worksheet was especially created for the CFA Review Program, and is not a part of the first version of *The Innovative Investor*. The structure of this worksheet resembles *Term Structure*. While the worksheet begins with newspaper quotes of bond prices and characteristics, it takes off in a different direction.

First, one can provide either yields or prices, and determine the other variable. Second, duration and convexity are computed for up to 12 bonds. The introductory screen below tells of the capabilities of the worksheet. This screen appears when you click the **Intro** button on the *Menu* screen.

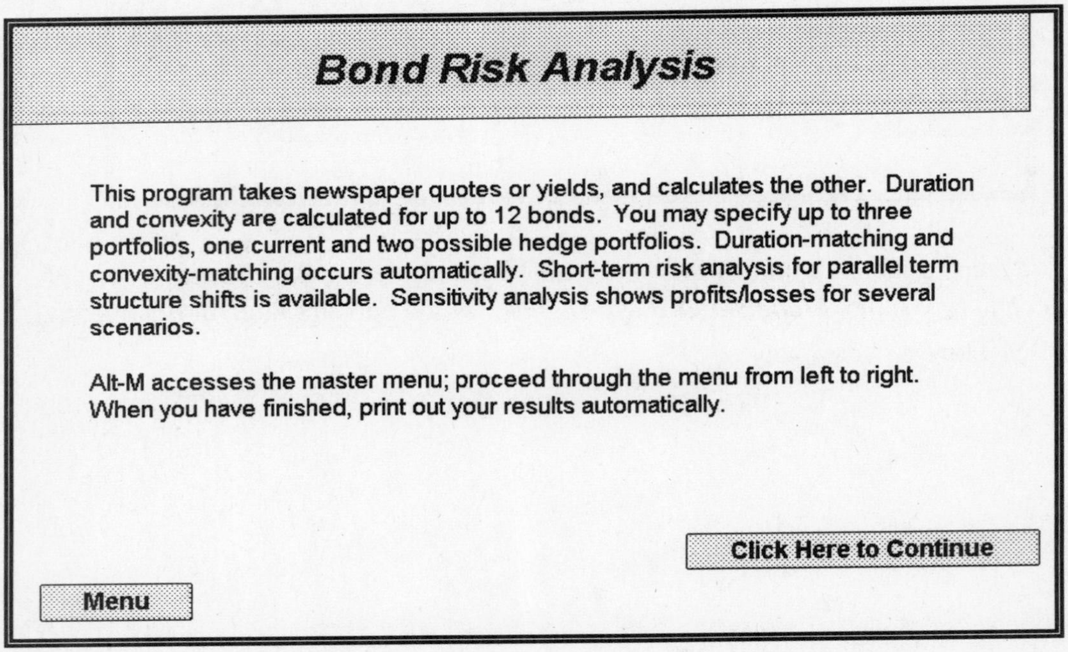
Bond Risk Analysis
This program takes newspaper quotes or yields, and calculates the other. Duration and convexity are calculated for up to 12 bonds. You may specify up to three portfolios, one current and two possible hedge portfolios. Duration-matching and convexity-matching occurs automatically. Short-term risk analysis for parallel term structure shifts is available. Sensitivity analysis shows profits/losses for several scenarios.
Alt-M accesses the master menu; proceed through the menu from left to right. When you have finished, print out your results automatically.
Click Here to Continue
Menu

Continue to the general instructions and background questions. Fill in the questions along the way by changing the highlighted numbers. Newspaper prices do not include accrued interest. You may start your analysis from today, or from any particular reference date you indicate.

INSTRUCTIONS and BACKGROUND INFORMATION

- Payments are assumed equally spaced throughout each year
- A payment is assumed to occur at maturity as well

This program can use newspaper quotes to calculate yield, duration, and volatility.
You can use today's date as a basis or the newspaper date (reference date).

Which date should I use as the reference date? -->	2
1-Today's Date	10-May-97
2-Reference Date*	17-Mar-89 <--
If you chose the reference date, enter the date with a double quote mark in the following format: "30-Jun-85	
Will you enter prices or yields? 1-Prices, 2-Yields	1
How many days per year should the program assume?	365
Should the program include accrued interest in the reported bond prices? (1-Yes, 2-No)	2

Click Here to Continue

As you continue, the *Bond Price and Coupon Information* screen requests information for up to 12 bonds. If you have indicated that you will supply prices (yields), then the program will indicate what it expects you to provide and what it expects to calculate. Once the requested data is entered, click the **Type Info Then Click Here to Compute** button to perform the calculations.

BOND PRICE and COUPON INFORMATION

Type Info Then Click Here to Compute

Bond #	Quote (Provide)	Ann Coupon	Pmts /Yr	Yield (Compute)	Pmt at Mat	Maturity Date*	Accrued Interest
1	99.96	11.25%	2	12.00%	$100	30-Mar-89	$5.22
2	98.43	6.38%	2	12.00%	$100	30-Jun-89	$1.35
3	79.67	7.12%	2	12.00%	$100	28-Feb-95	$0.36
4	113.20	14.37%	2	12.00%	$100	30-Aug-98	$0.65
5	70.40	6.88%	2	12.00%	$100	30-Apr-99	$2.61
6	83.51	9.25%	2	12.00%	$100	30-Jan-2000	$1.20
7	74.86	8.00%	2	12.00%	$100	30-Mar-2001	$3.72
8	98.27	11.75%	2	12.00%	$100	30-Jul-2003	$1.53
9	68.31	7.38%	2	12.00%	$100	30-Dec-2003	$1.57
10	83.21	9.63%	2	12.00%	$100	30-Apr-2005	$3.65
11	67.18	7.63%	2	12.00%	$100	30-Nov-2008	$2.27
12	119.14	14.50%	2	12.00%	$100	30-Dec-2010	$3.08

Click Here to Clear Data

Click Here to Continue

Menu

* e.g. '01-Jan-80, or '15-Jun-2010

The next screen displays the following results:

BOND SUMMARIES and STATISTICS

Bond #	Bond	Current Yield	Yld to Maturity	Duration	Modified Duration	Convexity
1	11.25s89	10.70%	12.00%	0.04	0.03	0.02
2	6.38s89	6.39%	12.00%	0.30	0.27	0.13
3	7.12s95	8.90%	12.00%	5.06	4.52	5.10
4	14.37s98	12.62%	12.00%	5.98	5.34	12.25
5	6.88s99	9.42%	12.00%	7.00	6.25	15.26
6	9.25s00	10.92%	12.00%	6.98	6.23	16.52
7	8.00s01	10.18%	12.00%	7.30	6.52	20.91
8	11.75s03	11.77%	12.00%	7.50	6.70	25.06
9	7.38s03	10.55%	12.00%	8.29	7.40	28.94
10	9.63s05	11.08%	12.00%	7.90	7.05	31.48
11	7.63s08	10.98%	12.00%	8.78	7.84	42.97
12	14.50s10	11.86%	12.00%	8.19	7.32	40.41

Menu

Click Here to Continue

In the next screen we may enter three bond positions: our portfolio and two candidate hedge portfolios.

PORTFOLIO INFORMATION

Portfolio Name:

Holdings:

Enter portfolio holdings here, i.e. the number of bonds held. To match duration, leave a "?" in either hedge portfolio. To match duration and convexity, place two "?"s.

Click Here to Match

#	Bond	Current	Hedge1	Hedge2
1	11.25s89	1.00	1.00	0.00
2	6.38s89	1.00	1.00	0.00
3	7.12s95	1.00	1.00	0.00
4	14.37s98	1.00	1.00	0.00
5	6.88s99	1.00	0.00	0.00
6	9.25s00	1.00	0.00	0.00
7	8.00s01	1.00	0.00	0.00
8	11.75s03	1.00	0.00	1.00
9	7.38s03	1.00	0.00	1.00
10	9.63s05	1.00	0.00	1.00
11	7.63s08	1.00	0.00	1.00
12	14.50s10	1.00	0.00	1.00

(Not value-weighted)		Current	Hedge1	Hedge2
	Overall duration:	5.29	2.51	7.22
	Overall convexity:	19.53	4.56	33.87

Click Here to Continue

Menu

We use the first hedge portfolio to duration match, and the second to match both duration and convexity. The question marks indicate the bond positions that may be altered.

PORTFOLIO INFORMATION

#	Bond	Portfolio Name:	Current	Hedge1	Hedge2
1	11.25s89	Holdings:	1.00	1.00	0.00
2	6.38s89		1.00	1.00	0.00
3	7.12s95	Enter portfolio holdings	1.00	1.00	0.00
4	14.37s98	here, i.e. the number of	1.00	1.00	0.00
5	6.88s99	bonds held. To match	1.00	?	0.00
6	9.25s00	duration, leave a "?" in	1.00	0.00	0.00
7	8.00s01	either hedge portfolio.	1.00	0.00	?
8	11.75s03	To match duration and	1.00	0.00	?
9	7.38s03	convexity, place two "?"s.	1.00	0.00	1.00
10	9.63s05		1.00	0.00	1.00
11	7.63s08	Click Here to Match	1.00	0.00	1.00
12	14.50s10		1.00	0.00	1.00
(Not value-weighted)		Overall duration:	5.29	2.51	7.37
		Overall convexity:	19.53	4.56	36.39

Menu

Click Here to Continue

Use the **Click Here to Match** button to determine the appropriate hedging weights (10.38 bond #5 for the first hedge portfolio, and 12.34 bond #7 together with -4.72 bond #8 for the second hedge portfolio.) We changed the hedge portfolios back to their original holdings. We now examine the short-term interest rate exposure of our portfolios, in particular, a 3% drop in interest rates across the board. What will happen to all our portfolios?

The graph of the unoptimized hedge position sensitivity appears on the next page.

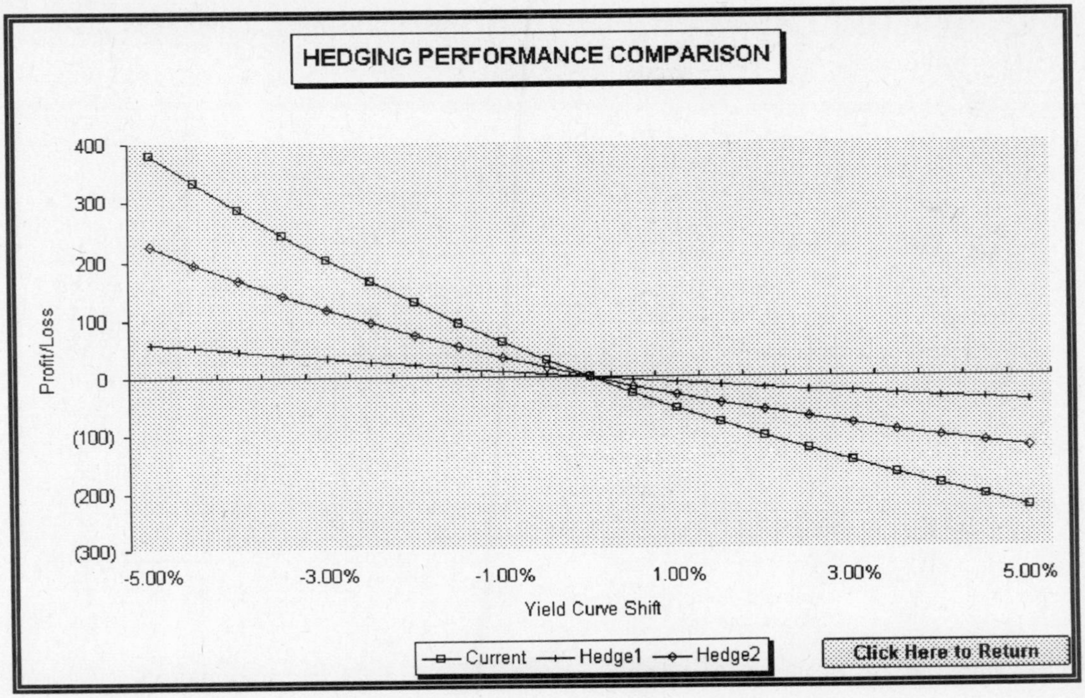
HEDGING PERFORMANCE COMPARISON
400
300
200
100
0
(100)
(200)
(300)
Profit/Loss
-5.00%
-3.00%
-1.00%
1.00%
3.00%
5.00%
Yield Curve Shift
Current
Hedge1
Hedge2
Click Here to Return

Verify that the optimized position shows better performance.

Portfolio Risk Exposures

Current Summary	Dur'n	Conv'y	Value	VxD	VxC
Current	5.29	19.53	1,083	5,733	21,154
Hedge1	2.51	4.56	399	1,000	1,817
Hedge2	7.22	33.87	448	3,237	15,181
----> Yield Curve Shift			-3.00%		
Projection	Dur'n	Conv'y	Value	VxD	VxC
Current	6.15	22.31	1,286	7,902	28,687
Hedge1	2.84	5.02	432	1,228	2,168
Hedge2	8.31	37.83	566	4,697	21,394
Profit/Loss			Dollars	Percent	
Current			202	18.68%	
Hedge1			33	8.35%	
Hedge2			117	26.19%	

The best picture of our interest rate risk can be seen in the next screen. Here is the table it produces:

Term Structure Shifts and Profits/Losses

TS Shift

Step 0.50%

Begin

Click Here to Graph

Click Here to Restart

Menu

	Current	Hedge1	Hedge2
-5.00%	380	60	225
-4.50%	332	53	195
-4.00%	286	46	168
-3.50%	243	40	142
-3.00%	202	33	117
-2.50%	164	27	95
-2.00%	128	21	73
-1.50%	93	16	53
-1.00%	60	10	34
-0.50%	29	5	17
0.00%	0	0	0
0.50%	(28)	(5)	(16)
1.00%	(55)	(10)	(31)
1.50%	(80)	(14)	(45)
2.00%	(104)	(19)	(58)
2.50%	(127)	(23)	(70)
3.00%	(149)	(27)	(82)
3.50%	(169)	(31)	(93)
4.00%	(189)	(35)	(104)
4.50%	(208)	(39)	(114)
5.00%	(226)	(43)	(123)

Test your understanding of this worksheet by completing the *Problems to Accompany Bond Risk Analysis*, which appears later in this manual.

Worksheet 5
Term Structure Analysis
Specific Instructions and a Numerical Example

TERMSTR.XLS

This worksheet is relatively straightforward. The user supplies newspaper quotes for bond prices, and from them generates a term structure of interest rates. The program calculates duration and volatility, and allows the user to prescribe duration or maturity as the independent variable in the term structure table. Once the term structure has been established, the user can discount cash flows of arbitrary patterns and find present values.

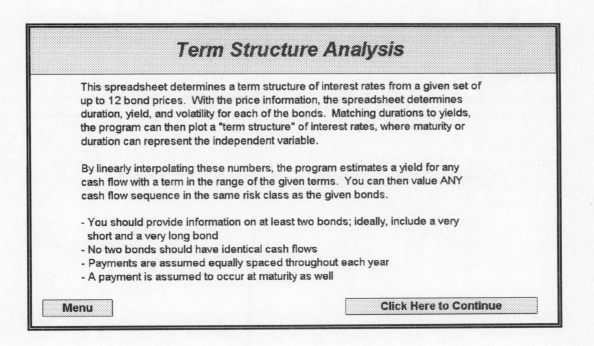

Term Structure Analysis

This spreadsheet determines a term structure of interest rates from a given set of up to 12 bond prices. With the price information, the spreadsheet determines duration, yield, and volatility for each of the bonds. Matching durations to yields, the program can then plot a "term structure" of interest rates, where maturity or duration can represent the independent variable.

By linearly interpolating these numbers, the program estimates a yield for any cash flow with a term in the range of the given terms. You can then value ANY cash flow sequence in the same risk class as the given bonds.

- You should provide information on at least two bonds; ideally, include a very short and a very long bond
- No two bonds should have identical cash flows
- Payments are assumed equally spaced throughout each year
- A payment is assumed to occur at maturity as well

Menu | Click Here to Continue

The following page of questions must be answered:

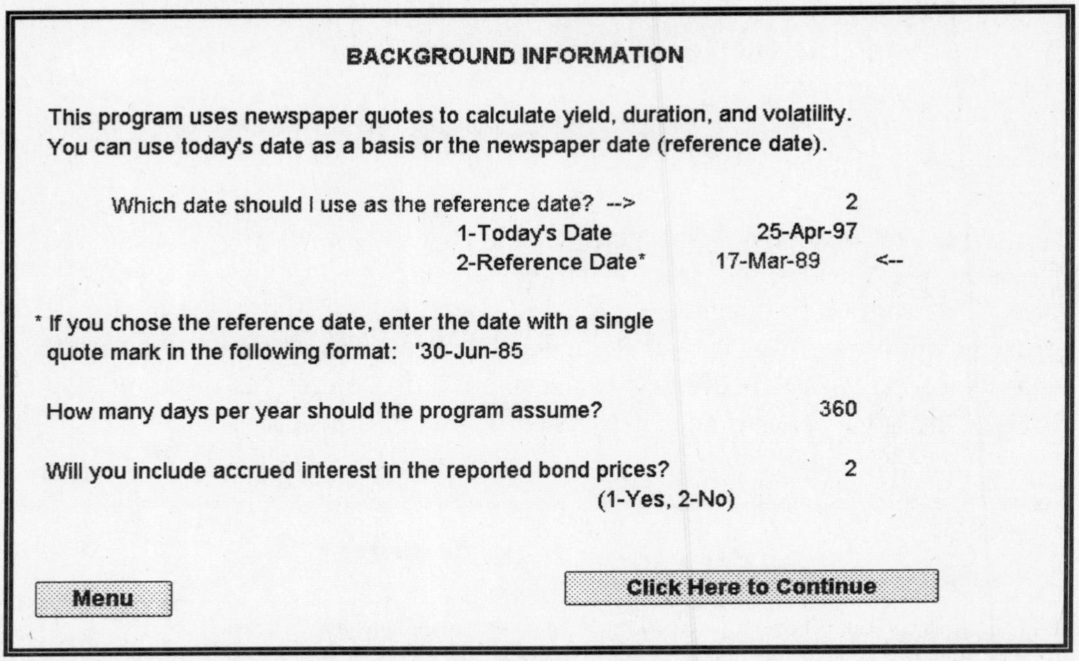
BACKGROUND INFORMATION
This program uses newspaper quotes to calculate yield, duration, and volatility.
You can use today's date as a basis or the newspaper date (reference date).
Which date should I use as the reference date? -->
2
1-Today's Date
25-Apr-97
2-Reference Date*
17-Mar-89
<--
* If you chose the reference date, enter the date with a single quote mark in the following format: '30-Jun-85
How many days per year should the program assume?
360
Will you include accrued interest in the reported bond prices?
2
(1-Yes, 2-No)
Menu
Click Here to Continue

The reference date indicates the date of the newspaper being used. If you would rather work with theoretical bond prices, simply choose a date like 01-Jan-00, and calculate maturity dates relative to that date. The advantage to this set-up is that it allows you to use newspaper quotes to determine the term structure.

Most newspaper quotes do not include accrued interest in the reported prices of bonds. Use the **Click Here to Continue** button to display the screen where you can supply the requisite data.

BOND PRICE and COUPON INFORMATION Type in your newspaper data

Bond Number	Quote (decimal)	Ann Coupon	Payments per Year	Size of Payment	Payment at Mat	Maturity Date*	Accrued Interest
1	100.125	0.1125	2	$5.63	$100	30-Mar-89	$5.22
2	99.9375	0.06375	2	$3.19	$100	30-Mar-89	$2.96
3	99.75	0.07125	2	$3.56	$100	30-Apr-89	$2.69
4	100.2813	0.14375	2	$7.19	$100	30-Apr-89	$5.43
5	99.59375	0.06875	2	$3.44	$100	30-May-89	$2.02
6	100	0.0925	2	$4.63	$100	30-May-89	$2.72
7	99.71875	0.08	2	$4.00	$100	30-May-89	$2.36
8	100.3438	0.1175	2	$5.88	$100	30-May-89	$3.46
9	99.4375	0.07375	2	$3.69	$100	30-Jun-89	$1.54
10	100.0313	0.09625	2	$4.81	$100	30-Jun-89	$2.01
11	99.3125	0.07625	2	$3.81	$100	30-Jul-89	$0.95
12	101.5	0.145	2	$7.25	$100	30-Jul-89	$1.81

Click Here to Clear Table **Click Here to Continue**

Menu * e.g. '01-Jan-80, or '15-Jun-2010

You may enter the quote as =100+1/8, as we did for bond number 1. Likewise the coupons for bond number 1 were entered as =11%+(1/4)%. The computer determined the size of each payment; check to make sure that it seems correct to you. The maturity date must be entered by preceding it with a quote mark; see the example at the bottom of the screen. Occasionally you may get a #DIV/0 message in some of the cells on later screens. If this happens try changing your maturity dates so that no two dates are the same. A day earlier or later does not significantly affect the results and eliminates the #DIV/0 messages. Now click the **Click Here to Continue** button to perform yield and duration calculations.

BOND SUMMARIES and STATISTICS **Click Here to Recalculate Yields**

Bond Number	Annual Coupon	Payments Remain	Next Payment	Current Yield	Yield to Maturity	Duration		Volatility
1	11.25%	1	30-Mar-89	10.68%	7.52%	0.04	#1	0.03
2	6.38%	1	30-Mar-89	6.20%	8.02%	0.04	#2	0.03
3	7.13%	1	30-Apr-89	6.96%	9.10%	0.12	#3	0.11
4	14.38%	1	30-Apr-89	13.60%	11.67%	0.12	#4	0.11
5	6.88%	1	30-May-89	6.77%	8.82%	0.21	#5	0.19
6	9.25%	1	30-May-89	9.00%	9.12%	0.21	#6	0.19
7	8.00%	1	30-May-89	7.84%	9.30%	0.21	#7	0.19
8	11.75%	1	30-May-89	11.32%	9.85%	0.21	#8	0.19
9	7.38%	1	30-Jun-89	7.30%	9.30%	0.29	#9	0.27
10	9.63%	1	30-Jun-89	9.43%	9.42%	0.29	#10	0.27
11	7.63%	1	30-Jul-89	7.60%	9.49%	0.38	#11	0.34
12	14.50%	1	30-Jul-89	14.04%	10.23%	0.38	#12	0.34

Menu **Click Here to Continue**

The program will automatically recalculate this screen if you reach it by clicking the **Click Here to Continue** button of the *Bond Price and Coupon Information* screen. If it seems to get into a perpetual loop, hit **CTRL-BREAK** twice to break out of it, and then double check the information you provided. You may not input any numbers on this screen; they are for study and reporting only.

The *Term Structure Calculation* screen asks whether you will plot yields by duration or by term. Both methods have their flaws: under term-plotting, varying coupon payments give the impression of multiple arbitrage opportunities when none might exist. Duration provides an approximate solution for the problem, but assumes that the term structure makes parallel vertical shifts only. Either way, the choice is yours; the term structure will be constructed as you wish.

TERM STRUCTURE CALCULATION

We now have all the information we need to calculate the term structure of interest rates. If you want to change any data, use the Menu button to return to the Menu screen. Then press the Market button to display the screen where you can enter new market data.

You may plot the term structure by maturity or by duration of the bonds. Please indicate your preference here:

Choice of Independent Variable: 2

1 - Time to Maturity

2 - Duration

Click Here to Continue

Menu

Term Structure Construction

	Yield	Duration	Bond #
1	10.23%	0.375	#12
2	9.49%	0.375	#11
3	9.30%	0.292	#9
4	9.42%	0.292	#10
5	8.82%	0.206	#5
6	9.12%	0.206	#6
7	9.85%	0.206	#8
8	9.30%	0.206	#7
9	9.10%	0.122	#3
10	11.67%	0.122	#4
11	7.52%	0.036	#1
12	8.02%	0.036	#2

The spreadsheet will now use these yields together with linear interpolation to estimate the yield on bonds of any duration.

With this information, you can find the present value of arbitrary cash flows knowing their discount rates from this term structure.

Click Here to Show Graph

Click Here to Continue

Menu

This is the graph produced by the worksheet:

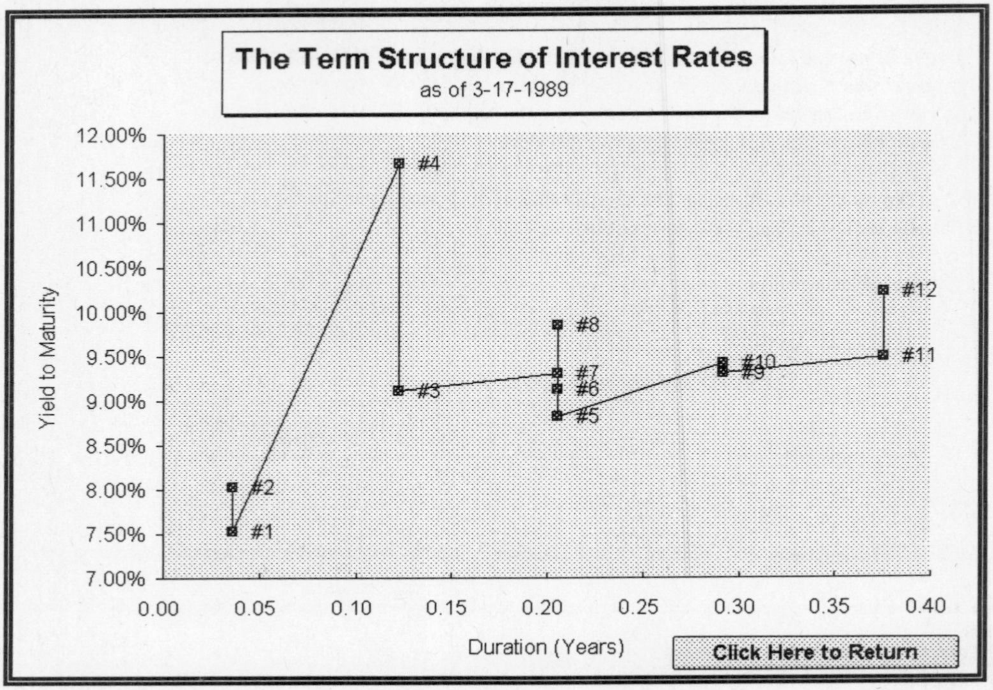
The Term Structure of Interest Rates
as of 3-17-1989
12.00%
11.50%
11.00%
10.50%
10.00%
9.50%
9.00%
8.50%
8.00%
7.50%
7.00%
Yield to Maturity
#1
#2
#3
#4
#5
#6
#7
#8
#9
#10
#11
#12
0.00
0.05
0.10
0.15
0.20
0.25
0.30
0.35
0.40
Duration (Years)
Click Here to Return

Click the **Click Here to Continue** button to value arbitrary cash flows under this term structure scenario. In this example, we have a 12.5 year annuity that starts making payments on Dec 14, 1988. Recall that the reference data was Sep 21, 1988, so that this makes sense. Payments are semiannual, and in the amount of $100 each.

Valuing Cash Flows with the Term Structure

You may now specify the cash flows of any annuity, or other arbitrary sequence of cash flows. With the cash flow information, we can discount at yields implied by your bond price data. Begin by supplying the annuity data.

ANNUITY DATA

Date of First Cash Flow*:	14-dec-88
Months between Payments:	6
Number of Payments (maximum 50 allowed)	25
Size of Payment:	$100

* (e.g., '6-Jun-92 or '3-May-2015)

Click Here to Continue

Menu

We can now input miscellaneous cash flows together with our annuity from above. For example, we could add a final principal repayment if we had a coupon-paying bond instead of an annuity.

Valuing Cash Flows with the Term Structure

Now you may indicate final cash flows associated with the annuity above, or any other arbitrary cash flows. When entering dates, use a single quote followed by the date, e.g. '6-Jun-89 or '30-May-2015 . Supply only the amounts and dates of cash flows.

OTHER CASH FLOWS

Amount	Date*	Yield	PV	Time (Years)
$40	14-dec-88	8.02%	$40.79	-0.25
$1,040	14-jun-89	9.09%	$1,018.19	0.24
		8.02%	$0.00	0.00
		8.02%	$0.00	0.00
		8.02%	$0.00	0.00
		8.02%	$0.00	0.00
		8.02%	$0.00	0.00

Menu | Click Here to Continue

The moment we've been waiting for!

Valuing Cash Flows with the Term Structure

FINAL RESULTS

	Term	Duration	Yield	Value
Annuity	11.75	4.51	10.23%	$1,518.22
Other	0.24	0.22	8.95%	$1,058.99
Total	11.75	2.75	10.23%	$2,577.21

The values given by this screen may be different than those produced by manual calculation or a bond calculator.

Click Here to Start Again

Menu

Ideally, this worksheet should provide a basis for making investment decisions; this present value should be compared with other present values to determine net value added of projects, or to identify arbitrage opportunities in the bond markets.

Test your understanding of this worksheet by completing the *Problems to Accompany Term Structure Analysis*, which appears later in this manual.

Worksheet 6
Quick Bond Valuation
Specific Instructions and a Numerical Example

QUIKBOND.XLS

This worksheet is designed to help the student experiment with bond-pricing concepts. The worksheet makes the limiting assumption that a coupon payment has just been made, or the bond has just been issued. In real life, we'd like to have more flexibility than this, but for teaching purposes this worksheet tells a lot. Not only do we learn about pricing and yield to maturity, but also about duration, modified duration, and convexity. The worksheet first prices individual bonds (or finds missing assumed values) and proceeds to do complex sensitivity analysis. The structure is general enough to apply to many bond-pricing problems a student will encounter.

The organization of the worksheet is similar to others in the package:

Menu: Click this button to return to the *Menu* screen

Intro: Introduction to the program (appearing below)

Background: Information for program computations

Calculations: The main calculation module

Sensitivity: Sensitivity analysis settings

What-If: Actual sensitivity analysis performed

Graph: Show sensitivity analysis graphically

Print: Print your results

Quit: Leave the main menu

The first and second screens provide detailed information on the capabilities of the worksheet.

Quick Bond Valuation

This spreadsheet values bonds under the assumption that a coupon payment has just been made, or the bond has just been issued. You can calculate prices, yields, duration, modified duration and convexity for the bond you use.

The spreadsheet enables you to perform rapid and accurate "What-if?" calculations, and show your results numerically or graphically. The results can be printed automatically.

Menu **Click Here to Continue**

The Valuation Model

We make the following assumptions:

A coupon payment has just been made, or the bond has just been issued.

Coupon payments are made regularly; the coupon equals the face value of the debt times the annual coupon rate divided by the number of payments per year.

A coupon accompanies the return of the principal payment.

Yield to maturity is reported as a BOND EQUIVALENT YIELD; it is equal to the periodic yield multiplied by the number of periods per year.

Menu **Click Here to Continue**

The worksheet calculates yield to maturity, so the user must specify a maximum acceptable pricing error. The yield to maturity function is more general than the worksheet's built-in function.

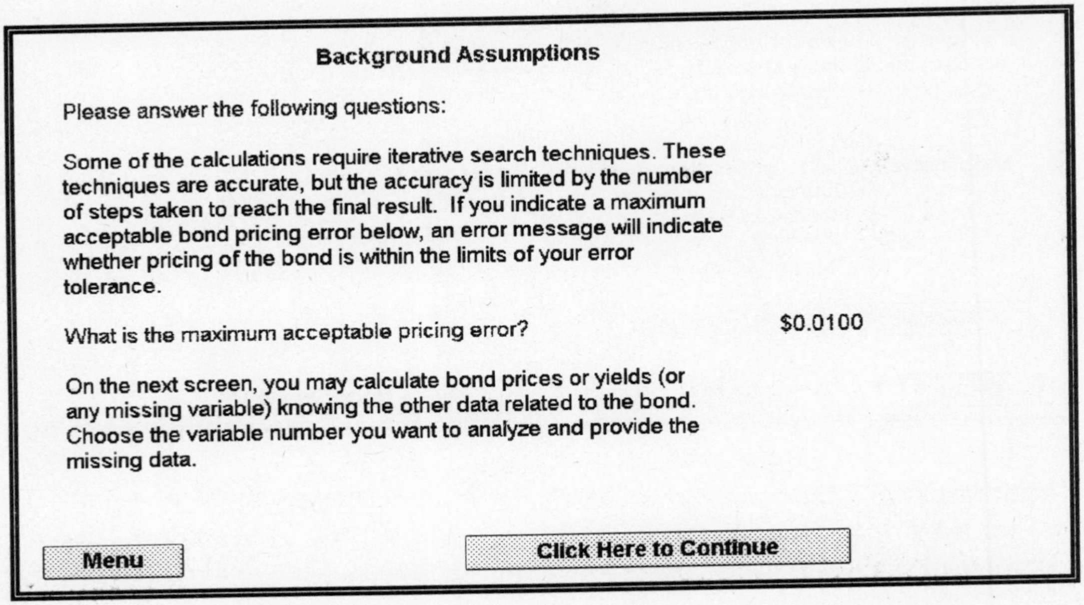
Background Assumptions
Please answer the following questions:
Some of the calculations require iterative search techniques. These techniques are accurate, but the accuracy is limited by the number of steps taken to reach the final result. If you indicate a maximum acceptable bond pricing error below, an error message will indicate whether pricing of the bond is within the limits of your error tolerance.
What is the maximum acceptable pricing error?
$0.0100
On the next screen, you may calculate bond prices or yields (or any missing variable) knowing the other data related to the bond. Choose the variable number you want to analyze and provide the missing data.
Menu
Click Here to Continue

The next page details the calculations involved in bond pricing — this is the core of the worksheet. First, choose the variable you want to calculate. Beginners will generally choose to calculate the bond price as a function of the other variables, face value, coupon rate, and so forth. More advanced users will want to calculate yield to maturity from price, or what coupon must be paid to reach a given yield.

The variable number appears to the left of the variable. Only variables 1–6 may be chosen here. Note that as you change the number of the variable you choose, the screen changes to show you where the result you desire will appear. In this case, the arrow points at selection 6. This implies that we should ignore the $1,119.50 figure, since it is supplied by the user. The price of the bond is read in the RESULT column, $1,160.46. You may wish to check this with your calculator to be certain.

Information and Calculations

Which variable would you like to calculate? 6

(fill in the DATA column, except for #6)

		DATA	RESULT
	1 - Face Value of Bond	$1,000.00	-----
	2 - Annual Coupon Rate (decimal)	13.00%	-----
	3 - Number of Payments per Year	2	-----
	4 - Years to Maturity	20.00	-----
	5 - Yield to Maturity (decimal)	11.00%	-----
---->	6 - Price of the Bond	$1,119.50	$1,160.46

Risk Calculations

7 - Duration	8.68
8 - Modified Duration	7.82
9 - Convexity	0.39
10 - Loss / 1% interest rate increase	$90.77

Click Here to Copy RESULT into DATA

Menu | **Click Here for Help** | **Click Here to Continue**

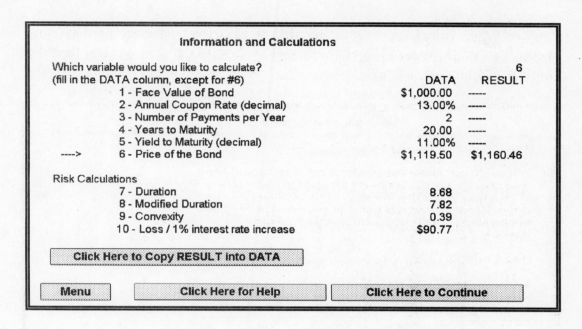

The program also reports duration, modified duration, convexity, and dollar loss for a 1% increase in interest rates. These concepts are explained somewhat in the HELP screen. Use the **Click Here for Help** button.

HELP!

What calculation is unknown (#1-6)? You must know five of the values to find the sixth. List the number of the variable you wish to calculate first; then fill in the five known values. The missing value appears in the column marked "RESULT."

The yield is a BOND EQUIVALENT YIELD, which is equal to the periodic yield times the number of payments per year.

The MODIFIED DURATION shows by what percentage the value of the bond will drop if interest rates increase across the board by 1%. The calculation is most accurate for small changes in the yield. CONVEXITY represents the amount by which the modified duration changes when yield increases by 1%. Finally, DURATION is the weighted average life of the bond's coupons. The value shown here is approximate; however, the approximation is usually accurate.

In the sensitivity analysis section, you may choose the variable you want to display on the horizontal axis. In this case, you may choose any of the 10 variables given in the following screen. I chose to study modified duration.

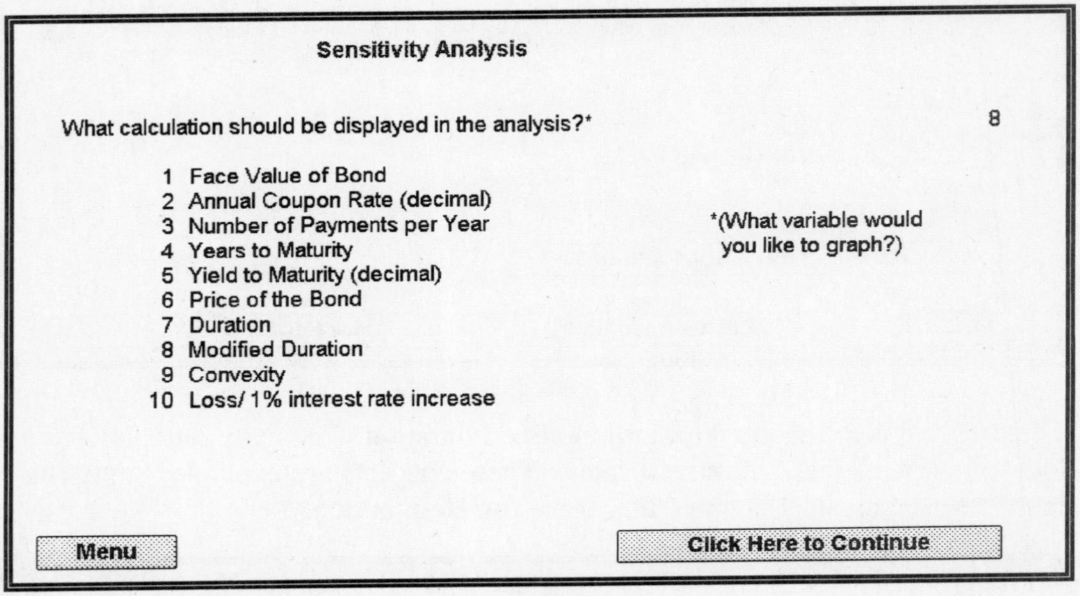
Sensitivity Analysis
What calculation should be displayed in the analysis?*
8
1 Face Value of Bond
2 Annual Coupon Rate (decimal)
3 Number of Payments per Year
4 Years to Maturity
5 Yield to Maturity (decimal)
6 Price of the Bond
7 Duration
8 Modified Duration
9 Convexity
10 Loss/ 1% interest rate increase
*(What variable would you like to graph?)
Menu
Click Here to Continue

The **Click Here to Continue** button displays the next screen. Choose the two most important variables in the sensitivity analysis. In this case, I want to vary yield to maturity and years to maturity and see the effect on modified duration. Skip the reference section, and then pick the steps for your variables. When you put in a number on the right, the text on the left changes to show you the effect.

Sensitivity Analysis for Modified Duration

		Major	Minor
Variable Importance		Major	Minor
What variables can change in the analysis?		5	4
Reference: Current values of the variables			C|
-1-	Face Value of Bond	$1,000.00	h|
-2-	Annual Coupon Rate	0.13	a|
-3-	Payments per Year	2	n|
-4-	Number of Years	20	g|
-5-	Yield to Maturity	11.00%	e|
-6-	Price of the Bond	$1,160.46	V

Size for 'Yield to Maturity' Increments: 0.02
(9 values altogether, from 0.03 to 0.19)
Size for 'Number of Years' Increments: 3
(5 values altogether, from 14.00 to 26.00)

Menu | Click Here for Help | Click Here to Continue

Again, for your reference, a HELP! screen is provided.

HELP!

How do you want the sensitivity analysis to look?
The MAJOR VARIABLE runs along the X-axis, and the OUTPUT VARIABLE (that you chose in the previous screen) runs along the Y-axis. The MINOR VARIABLE effects are shown with different lines in the graph.

NOTE: Check the INCREMENTS (Steps) to make sure that each variable is given an appropriate range. You can check to see if the range is correct by looking at the rows:

(9 values altogether ...)
(5 values altogether ...)

The assumptions on the other inputs are shown for reference only.

On the next screen, *What-if?*, click the **Click Here to Recalculate** button to actually perform the sensitivity analysis you indicated.

Sensitivity Analysis
(Sensitivity Analysis Completed for Modified Duration)

Number of Years

Yield to Maturity	14.00	17.00	20.00	23.00	26.00
3.00%	8.86	10.21	11.46	12.64	13.76
5.00%	8.34	9.47	10.48	11.39	12.22
7.00%	7.83	8.75	9.54	10.21	10.79
9.00%	7.33	8.06	8.65	9.12	9.51
11.00%	6.84	7.40	7.82	8.14	8.37
13.00%	6.37	6.79	7.07	7.27	7.40
15.00%	5.93	6.22	6.40	6.51	6.57
17.00%	5.51	5.71	5.81	5.86	5.88
19.00%	5.13	5.24	5.28	5.29	5.29

Click Here to Recalculate (if necessary)

Menu

Click Here to Continue

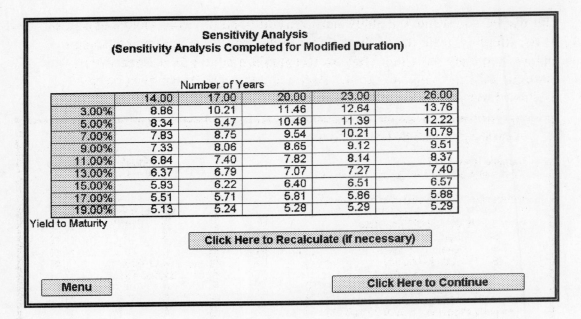

Return to the *Menu* screen and click the **Graph** button to view a graph of these results.

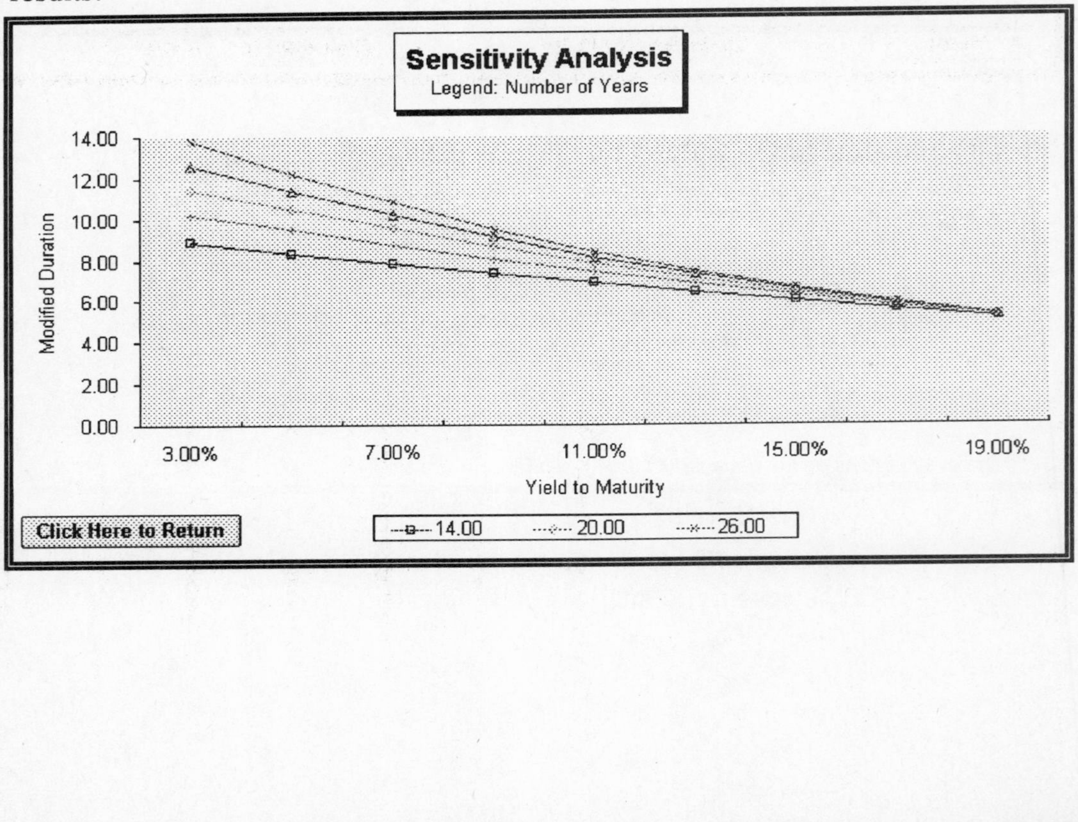
Sensitivity Analysis
Legend: Number of Years
14.00
12.00
10.00
8.00
6.00
4.00
2.00
0.00
Modified Duration
3.00%
7.00%
11.00%
15.00%
19.00%
Yield to Maturity
Click Here to Return
14.00
20.00
26.00

But maybe you wanted to study sensitivity of bond prices to yield and coupon. If so, simply change the study variable to #6, revise the parameters screen below, and click the **Click Here to Recalculate** button on the *Sensitivity Analysis* screen. You can use the **Page Up** and **Page Down** keys on the keyboard to cycle between these screens.

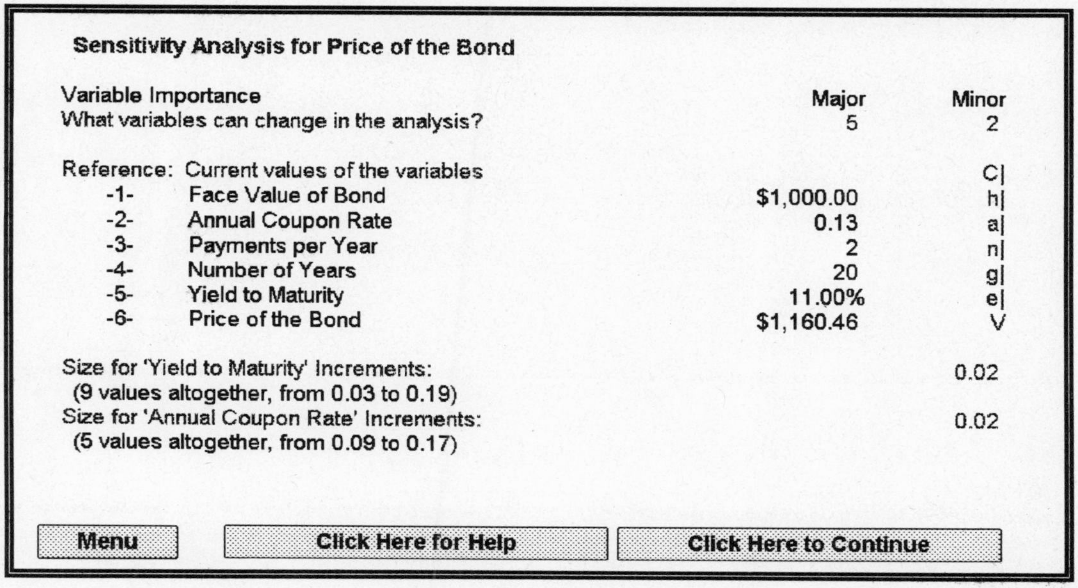
Sensitivity Analysis for Price of the Bond
Variable Importance
What variables can change in the analysis?
Major
5
Minor
2
Reference: Current values of the variables
-1- Face Value of Bond $1,000.00
-2- Annual Coupon Rate 0.13
-3- Payments per Year 2
-4- Number of Years 20
-5- Yield to Maturity 11.00%
-6- Price of the Bond $1,160.46
C| h| a| n| g| e| V
Size for 'Yield to Maturity' Increments: 0.02
(9 values altogether, from 0.03 to 0.19)
Size for 'Annual Coupon Rate' Increments: 0.02
(5 values altogether, from 0.09 to 0.17)
Menu
Click Here for Help
Click Here to Continue

The corresponding graph follows on the next page.

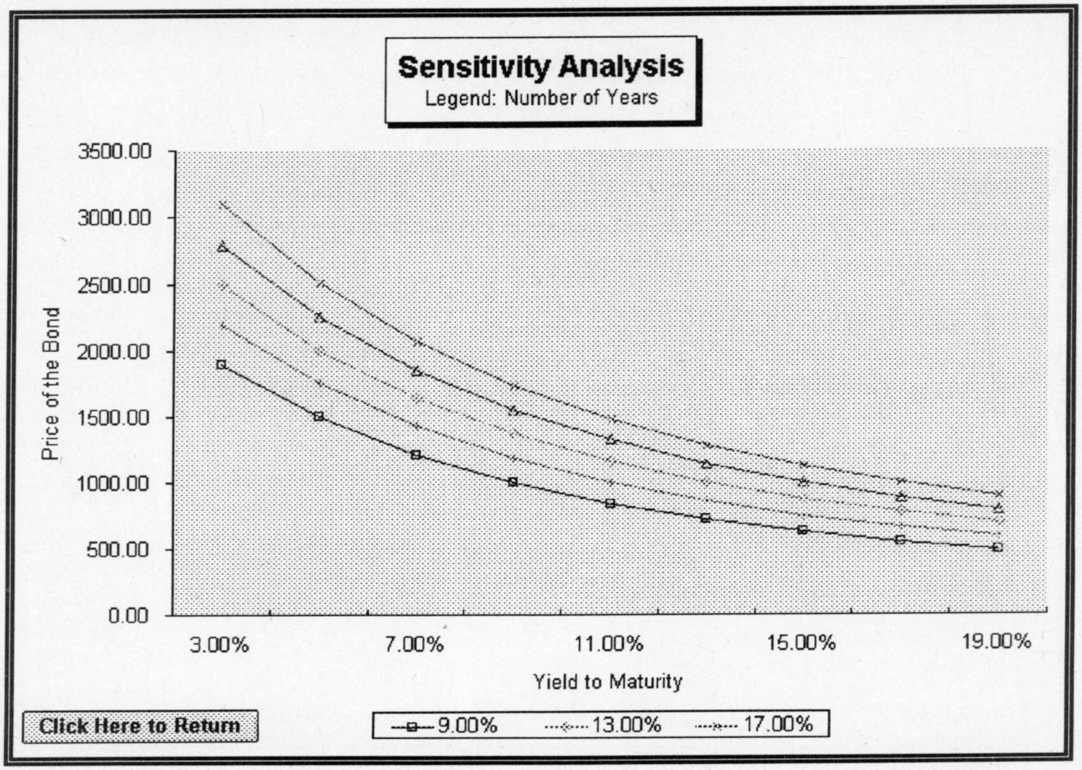
Sensitivity Analysis
Legend: Number of Years
3500.00
3000.00
2500.00
2000.00
1500.00
1000.00
500.00
0.00
Price of the Bond
3.00%
7.00%
11.00%
15.00%
19.00%
Yield to Maturity
Click Here to Return
9.00%
13.00%
17.00%

Test your understanding of this worksheet by completing the *Problems to Accompany Quick Bond Valuation*, which appears later in this manual.

Worksheet 7
Valuing Convertible Debt
Specific Instructions and a Numerical Example

CONVPRIC. XLS

Much of the documentation for this program, along with the discussion questions themselves, is included in the body of the program. The program allows you to value convertible discount bonds and callable convertible discount bonds using the model of Jon Ingersoll, Jr.

The worksheet introduction:

Valuing Convertible Debt

This spreadsheet values a few specific complex debt instruments under some restrictive assumptions. The formulations follow a paper by Jon Ingersoll, Jr, entitled "A Contingent Claims Valuation of Convertible Securities", which appeared in the Journal of Financial Economics, v.4, 1977, pp. 289-322.

In order to derive exact solutions for the value of callable bonds, convertible bonds, and callable convertible bonds, Ingersoll made the following important assumptions (among others):

(1) Bonds make no coupon payments
(2) The term structure is flat;
(3) The interest rate is constant;
(4) There is a single senior debt issue in the firm's capital structure.

Menu **Click Here to Continue**

In spite of the harsh nature of the assumptions, we can learn something about

(a) The valuation of convertible securities
(b) the optimal exercise strategy for convertible securities, whether exercise takes place on the part of the firm (CALL) or on the part of the bondholder (CONVERSION).

Spreadsheet designed by Los Angeles, California.

ADVANCED FINANCIAL SOFTWARE, INC.,

and

Richard D. Irwin, Inc., 1992.

Menu

Click Here to Continue

The worksheet begins by making the assumptions above, and then asking you, as the investor, to supply the relevant inputs to the bond pricing problem. The worksheet will take your inputs and determine the bond prices from them in the following two screens. Click the **Click Here to Continue** button to display the first screen for inputs.

VALUING CONVERTIBLE DEBT

Change the parameter values below to determine their impact on the valuation of convertible securities. For help interpreting parameter values, **Click Here** for an explanation.

Current Firm Value	$446.00
Value Volatility (annual pct std deviation)	50.0%
Maturity Date (years)	5
Face Value of Debt	$100.00
Interest rate (annual, as a decimal)	13.0%
Dilution Factor	15.0%
Call Price Disc Rate	8.0%
(Call Price discount rate implies Call Price of	$67.03)

Menu **Click Here to Continue**

The **Click Here** button displays the *Help with Parameter Values* screen with explanations for each of the input items.

HELP WITH PARAMETER VALUES

The FIRM VALUE represents the total value of the assets of the firm. As such, it includes both the equity and the debt of the firm.

The VOLATILITY represents the total annual volatility in percentage terms of the firm's assets.

The MATURITY DATE, FACE VALUE of the DEBT, and INTEREST RATE are exactly like those of any other discount bond.

The DILUTION FACTOR represents the proportion of the firm the bondholders WOULD own if they decided to convert their bonds.

The CALL PRICE DISCOUNT RATE represents the rate at which the firm discounts the face value to determine what they have to pay the bondholders if they decide to call the issue. This rate should normally be lower than the interest rate.

Display the *Results* screen by clicking the **Click Here to Continue** button on the input screen.

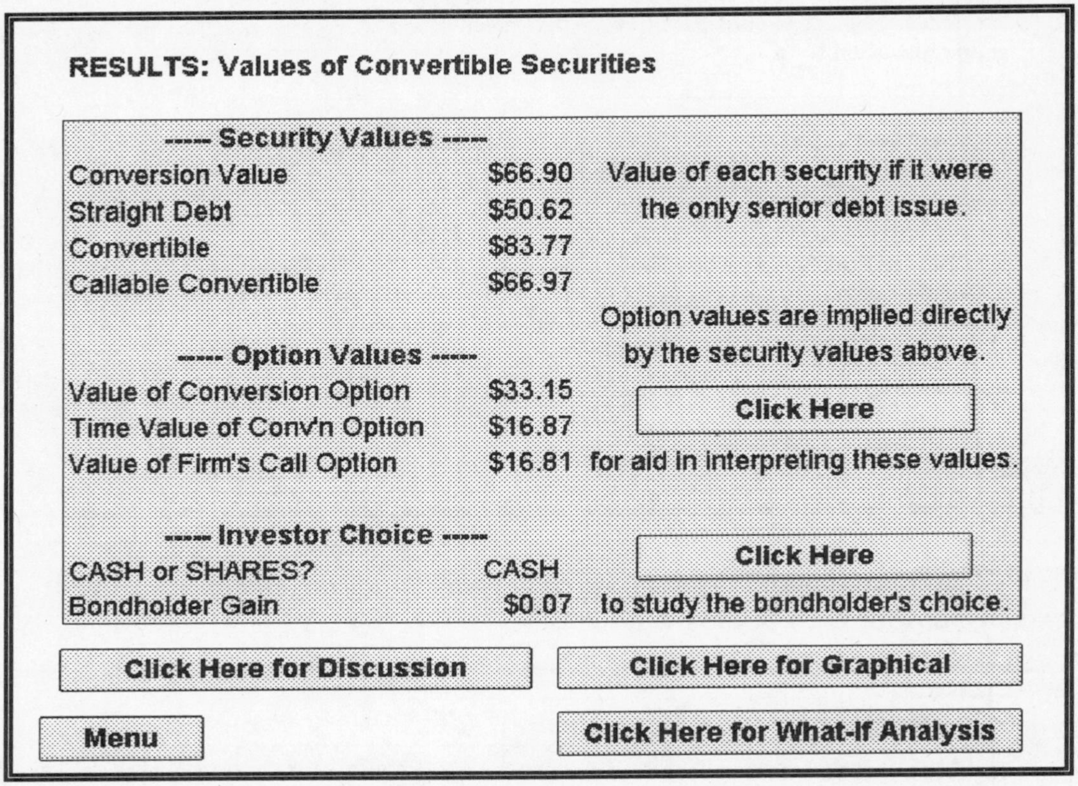
RESULTS: Values of Convertible Securities
----- Security Values -----
Conversion Value $66.90
Straight Debt $50.62
Convertible $83.77
Callable Convertible $66.97
Value of each security if it were the only senior debt issue.
Option values are implied directly by the security values above.
----- Option Values -----
Value of Conversion Option $33.15
Time Value of Conv'n Option $16.87
Value of Firm's Call Option $16.81
Click Here
for aid in interpreting these values.
----- Investor Choice -----
CASH or SHARES? CASH
Bondholder Gain $0.07
Click Here
to study the bondholder's choice.
Click Here for Discussion
Click Here for Graphical
Menu
Click Here for What-If Analysis

The program calculates the value of each bond in isolation:

If you need help at any time, plenty is supplied. The upper **Click Here** provides information about interpreting the results; the lower **Click Here** button provides help in understanding the Investor's Choice, "Should I take the cash for the call of the callable convertible, or should I convert?" The full text of these help screens appears on the following pages.

HELP WITH INTERPRETATION

The CONVERSION VALUE is the value of a convertible bond if it is converted now.

The STRAIGHT DEBT value is the value of a pure discount bond with no options attached.

THE CONVERTIBLE DEBT value is the value of the straight debt plus the value of the right to convert the debt to equity. Therefore, the value of the conversion option equals the difference between the values of the straight and convertible debt.

The CALLABLE CONVERTIBLE DEBT value is the value of the straight debt plus the value of the conversion option minus the value of the firm's call option. Therefore, the value of the call option equals the difference between the values of the convertible and the callable convertible.

We now wish to study the investor's choice under a callable convertible bond. Here is the help screen; to get the balance sheet, click the **Click Here** button.

HELP WITH the INVESTOR's CHOICE

The INVESTOR's CHOICE reflects the rational choice of an investor who, when called, must choose between taking cash (the call price) and shares of stock (the conversion value). The bondholder's gain shows what the bondholders gain in value if the firm decides to call now.

Click Here to see a balance sheet reflecting the change in the distribution of the firm's wealth as a result of a decision to call the debt. Sometimes the debtholder's stake becomes equity, while at other times she is paid in cash.

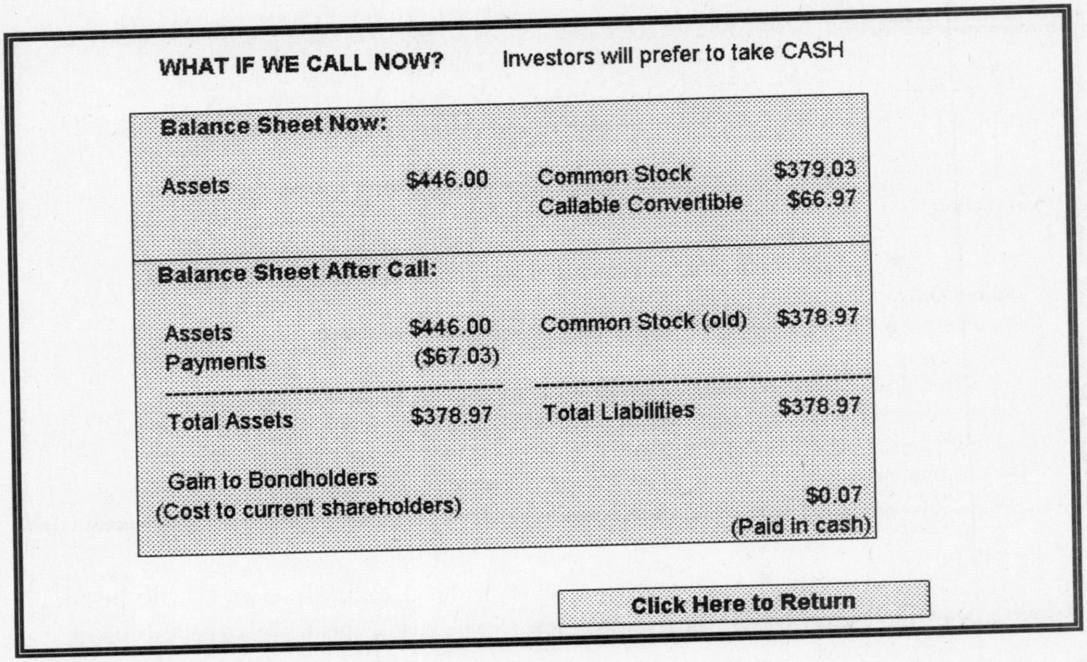
WHAT IF WE CALL NOW?
Investors will prefer to take CASH
Balance Sheet Now:
Assets
$446.00
Common Stock
$379.03
Callable Convertible
$66.97
Balance Sheet After Call:
Assets
$446.00
Payments
($67.03)
Common Stock (old)
$378.97
Total Assets
$378.97
Total Liabilities
$378.97
Gain to Bondholders
(Cost to current shareholders)
$0.07
(Paid in cash)
Click Here to Return

Note that the balance sheet changes whenever the underlying parameters change. The return buttons make it easy to switch between these related screens so you may experiment with different input values.

To see the bondholder's gains as a function of the stock price, click the **Gains** button on the *Menu* screen. The graph produced under the above assumptions can be seen on the next page.

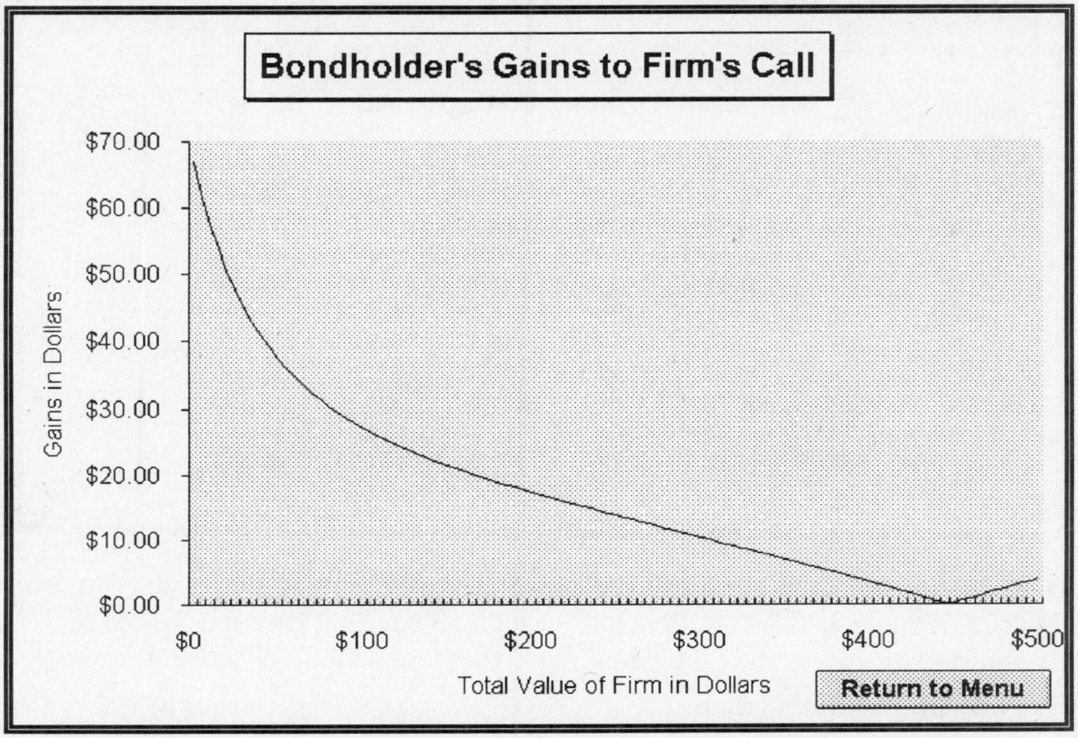
Bondholder's Gains to Firm's Call
$70.00
$60.00
$50.00
$40.00
$30.00
$20.00
$10.00
$0.00
Gains in Dollars
$0
$100
$200
$300
$400
$500
Total Value of Firm in Dollars
Return to Menu

Now we want to ask the question, "How are the bonds affected differently by changes in parameter values, particularly the underlying stock value?" To see the answer, click the **What-if?** button on the *Menu* screen or the **Click Here for What-if Analysis** on the *Results* screen.

What-if Analysis --- Securities vs. Firm Value | Click Here to Return

Click Here to View / Click Here to Recalc		Conv Value	Straight Debt	Non-call Conv	Callable Conv	B'holder Gain
Step\Min	$0	$0.00	$0.00	$0.00	$0.00	$67.03
$5	$5	$0.75	$4.90	$4.90	$4.90	$62.13
	$10	$1.50	$9.30	$9.30	$9.30	$57.73
	$15	$2.25	$13.13	$13.13	$13.13	$53.90
Value	$20	$3.00	$16.44	$16.46	$16.45	$50.59
of	$25	$3.75	$19.33	$19.37	$19.34	$47.69
Firm	$30	$4.50	$21.85	$21.93	$21.87	$45.16
(MAX:)	$35	$5.25	$24.08	$24.20	$24.12	$42.92
$500	$40	$6.00	$26.07	$26.24	$26.11	$40.92
	$45	$6.75	$27.84	$28.08	$27.90	$39.13

Only the top few rows are displayed above. On your spread sheet, you can use the up and down arrow keys to scroll through all rows of the data. To see a graphical expression, click the **Click Here to View** button. This action results in the graph below:

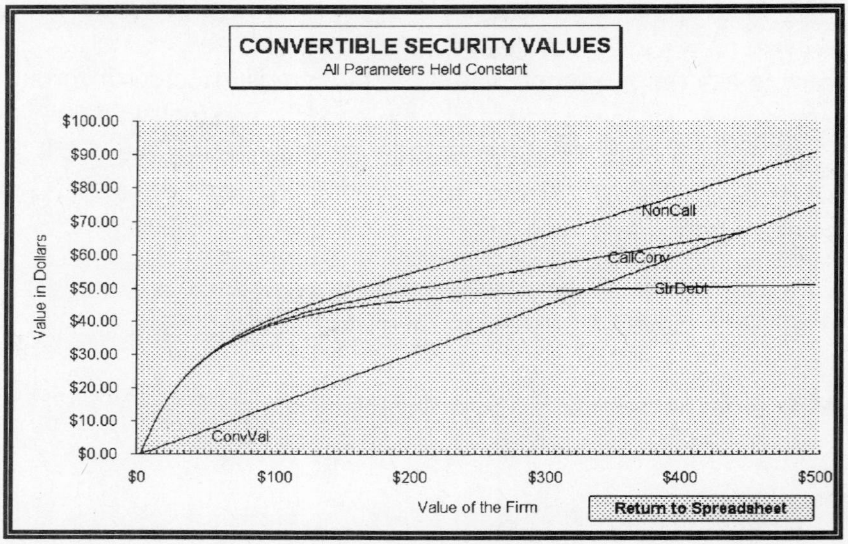
CONVERTIBLE SECURITY VALUES
All Parameters Held Constant
$100.00
$90.00
$80.00
$70.00
$60.00
$50.00
$40.00
$30.00
$20.00
$10.00
$0.00
Value in Dollars
NonCall
CallConv
StrDebt
ConvVal
$0
$100
$200
$300
$400
$500
Value of the Firm
Return to Spreadsheet

Finally, the worksheet asks you to test your understanding of concepts involving valuation of convertible securities.

QUESTIONS on GRAPHICAL INTERPRETATION

(1) Which of the three securities is always worth the most? Why?

(2) Why is the straight bond always worth the least? In other words, why can't the value of the _______ option ever exceed the value of the ______ option?

(3) At what firm value should the firm's management call the callable convertible debt?

(4) If the firm has issued convertible debt, and suddenly issues more (with exactly the same terms), what will happen to the diagram?

(5) How does an increase in the volatility of the firm's assets affect the values of convertible securities? Print a graph under two different volatility scenarios.

QUESTIONS for DISCUSSION

(A) Start with an asset value of $200, volatility 50%, maturity date 10 years, $100 face valued debt, a 13% interest rate, a 15% dilution factor, and an 8% call price discount rate. If the firm has issued callable convertibles, and calls now, what will the bondholders prefer to choose, cash or shares? Why?

(B) Print out the balance sheet associated with A. Calculate the value of the bondholders' gains, explain where those gains came from and why they took place.

(C) Suppose the firm's value jumps to $400 because of a new discovery. Repeat steps A and B.

(D) At what firm value should the company have called the debt? (This may take some experimentation) What is the bondholder's gain in this case? Can you justify your answer intuitively?

Use the **Graphical** or **Discussion** buttons on the *Menu* screen to display the screens represented above.

Test your understanding of this worksheet by completing the *Problems to Accompany Valuing Convertible Debt*, which appears later in this manual.

Worksheet 8
Two-Dividend Growth Model
Specific Instructions and a Numerical Example

TWODIV.XLS

This worksheet allows the student to perform two important tasks — the understanding and usage of the two-stage dividend growth model for equity valuation, and the ability to use market data to test stock selection theories. The valuation model here is quite flexible. One cannot only import data on 100 securities, but use the data to perform valuations. Alternatively, if the value is known, the assumptions leading to the results can be recovered. For example, if the final dividend growth rate is unknown, this worksheet will determine which final dividend growth rate makes the theoretical share price equal to the market you provide.

We would like to thank Market Base, Inc., for supplying the data used in this program. Data were provided on 100 securities; there are 12 balance sheets available for each security.

The capabilities of the program are summarized in the menu listing below:

Menu:	Worksheet menu
Intro:	Introduction to the program
Calcs:	Determine missing variable from set of five
Actual:	Use actual balance sheet data from 100 securities
Sensitivity:	Set parameters and determine model comparative statics
What-if?:	Recalculate What-if table
Graph:	Graphs sensitivity analysis results
Print:	Prints selected ranges

The *Menu* screen can be reached any time by clicking the **Menu** button. You can begin your analysis by clicking the **Intro** button. The *Intro* screen is followed by two more description screens, which appear on the following pages.

EQUITY VALUATION: The Two-Dividend Growth Model

This spreadsheet values stocks under the assumption that we know the value of the next dividend to be paid, and we have also made an intermediate dividend forecast. (Alternatively, we can specify a preliminary growth rate until the intermediate dividend.) Dividends are assumed to accrue perpetually at a given long-run growth rate. The valuation model discounts dividends at a constant rate to arrive at the share price.

With this spreadsheet, you can specify which four of the five values you know... the spreadsheet will automatically calculate the missing value. You may price shares of stock from today or a given reference date; incremental discounting takes place automatically.

Menu **Click Here to Continue**

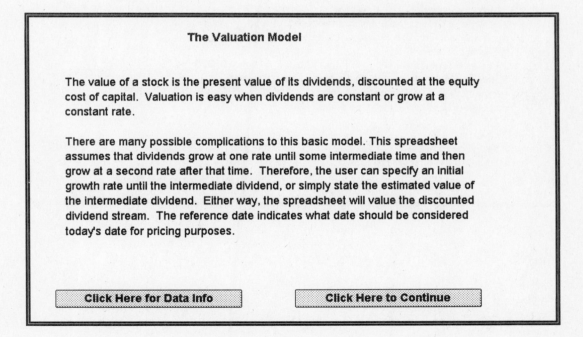

The Valuation Model

The value of a stock is the present value of its dividends, discounted at the equity cost of capital. Valuation is easy when dividends are constant or grow at a constant rate.

There are many possible complications to this basic model. This spreadsheet assumes that dividends grow at one rate until some intermediate time and then grow at a second rate after that time. Therefore, the user can specify an initial growth rate until the intermediate dividend, or simply state the estimated value of the intermediate dividend. Either way, the spreadsheet will value the discounted dividend stream. The reference date indicates what date should be considered today's date for pricing purposes.

Click Here for Data Info **Click Here to Continue**

The background screen next asks you how to set up the worksheet. This is a two-stage dividend growth model, so you must decide if you have an actual dividend forecast available before the mature growth stage is reached, or whether you want to work with an intermediate growth rate until that dividend forecast. The reference date calculation allows you to value the security at any time, now, in the past, or in the future. The pricing error tells the program to let you know when pricing is off by more than that error. This is necessary when iterative (search) techniques are used. Chances are, your valuations will always be within a reasonable error tolerance.

The CAPM data is used to determine the expected return on the security. Of course, the CAPM need not be true in order to use this worksheet — you may use any discount rate you like in the valuations. Click the **Click Here to Continue** button to display the *Valuation* screen.

Background Assumptions

Please answer the following questions:

Which data would you prefer to supply?			2
1 - Intermediate Dividend Forecast			
2 - Dividend Growth Rate until Intermediate Dividend			
Which date should I use as a reference date?			2
1 - Today's Date	15-Jul-97		
2 - Your Reference Date*	1-Apr-91	33329	
* Start your reference date with a single quote	'01-Jan-80		
How many days shall I assume per year?			365
What is the maximum acceptable pricing error?			$0.01

CAPM DATA:

Risk-free interest rate	5.00%	Beta	0.60
Expected return on market portfolio	11.00%	Discount Rate	8.60%

Click Here to Continue

At this point, you choose values for the economic variables in your model — for example, "How long is the initial growth stage? When is the first dividend expected to be paid?"

Where the program asks what value to calculate, indicate the variable number you want to work with. In this case, we want to calculate the value of the stock, given the other assumptions. Therefore, we placed a **1** in the variable box and provided data for the other variables. Note that the calculated stock price is shown in the right column. Ignore the $51.62 in the left column. However, if you change the variable number under consideration, the worksheet calculates the implied value of the variable that makes the market price equal to $51.62.

Information and Calculations

Date of first dividend — 1-Apr-92
(enter date w/single quote: '31-Dec-95 or '20-Aug-2010) — 33695

Number of dividend periods per year — 1
In what period does the intermediate dividend occur? — 4
(i.e., in 4.00 years from date of first dividend)
Which variable would you like to calculate?* — 1

(fill in the DATA column, except for #1)		DATA	RESULT
---->	1 - Value of Stock	51.62	83.00
	2 - First Dividend Projection	$2.49	-----
(Ann)	3 - Growth Rate until Intermediate	19.57%	-----
(Ann)	4 - Final Dividend Growth Rate	4.20%	-----
(Ann)	5 - Discount Rate	8.60%	-----

*Same as output variable in sensitivity analysis.

Menu — Click Here to Continue

We can use actual data by clicking the **Actual** button on the *Menu* screen. **IMPORTANT NOTE:** The only figure that can be modified on this page is the *Growth rate multiplier*, which can be used to reduce unusually high estimates of long-term growth. We chose AMOCO (Selection #10), but you can work with any of the stocks listed on the second page following:

Individual Stock Data from MARKET BASE Database

0	Selection number	10		
1	NAME:	AMOCO CORP	CALCULATED VALUES	
2	TICKER:	AN	Div payout	46.64%
3	PR:	51.62	Div yield	4.03%
4	BK:	28.92	ROE	15.74%
5	TAS:	30968	Growth rate multiplier	0.50
6	LTD:	10546	Price	51.62
7	SALES:	63.7	1st dividend forecast	$2.49
8	FCF:	1.65	Short-term growth	19.57%
9	VRE:	1.36	Final growth rte (adj)	4.20%
10	BETA:	0.6	Req'd rate (CAPM)	8.60%
11	DIV:	2.08	Final growth rte (raw)	8.40%
12	EPS2:	3.12	Valuation date	1-Apr-91
13	EPS1:	3.77	One-year out	1-Apr-92
14	EPS:	4.46		

Menu | Feed Data to the Spreadsheet

Click the **Feed Data to the Spreadsheet** to feed data from any security you choose into the worksheet. By returning to the *Information and Calculations* screen, you can overwrite any assumptions you find unreasonable.

Listing of Available Securities Data provided by Market Base, Inc.					
	COMPANY NAME	TICKER		COMPANY NAME	TICKER
1	ABBOTT LABORATORIES	ABT	51	KELLOGG CO	K
2	ALBERTSONS INC	ABS	52	KIMBERLY CLARK CORP	KMB
3	ALUMINUM CO OF AMERICA	AA	53	LIMITED INC	LTD
4	AMERICAN BRANDS	AMB	54	M C I COMM CORP	MCIC
5	AMERICAN CYANAMID CO	ACY	55	MAY DEPARTMENT STORES CO	MA
6	AMERICAN ELECTRIC POWER	AEP	56	MCDONALDS CORP	MCD
7	AMERICAN HOME PRODUCTS	AHP	57	MELVILLE CORP	MES
8	AMERICAN INFO TECH	AIT	58	MERCK & CO INC	MRK
9	AMERICAN TEL & TEL	T	59	MINNESOTA MINING & MFG	MMM
10	AMOCO CORP	AN	60	MOBIL CORP	MOB
11	ANHEUSER BUSCH COMPANIES	BUD	61	MONSANTO CO	MTC
12	APPLE COMPUTER INC	AAPL	62	MOTOROLA INC	MOT
13	ARCHER DANIELS MIDLAND CO	ADM	63	N C R CORP	NCR
14	ATLANTIC RICHFIELD CO	ARC	64	NORFOLK SOUTHERN CORP	NSC
15	BELL ATLANTIC CORP	BEL	65	NORTHERN TELECOM	NT
16	BELLSOUTH CORP	BLS	66	NYNEX CORP	NYN
17	BOEING CO	BA	67	P P G INDUSTRIES INC	PPG
18	BRISTOL MYERS SQUIBB	BMY	68	PACIFIC GAS & ELECTRIC CO	PCG
19	BURLINGTON RESOURCES	BR	69	PACIFIC TELESIS GROUP	PAC
20	CAMPBELL SOUP CO	CPB	70	PEPSICO	PEP
21	CAPITAL CITIES/ABC INC	CCB	71	PFIZER INC	PFE
22	CHEVRON CORP	CHV	72	PHILIP MORRIS COS INC	MO
23	COCA COLA CO	KO	73	PHILLIPS PETROLEUM CO	P
24	CONAGRA	CAG	74	PITNEY BOWES	PBI
25	CONSD EDISON OF NY	ED	75	PROCTER & GAMBLE CO	PG
26	COOPER INDUSTRIES	CBE	76	RALSTON PURINA CO	RAL
27	CORNING INC	GLW	77	RAYTHEON CO	RTN
28	DISNEY CO (WALT)	DIS	78	ROCKWELL INTL CORP	ROK
29	DOW CHEMICAL CO	DOW	79	S C E CORP	SCE
30	DU PONT DE NEMOURS & CO	DD	80	SARA LEE CORP	SLE
31	DUKE POWER CO	DUK	81	SCHERING PLOUGH CORP	SGP
32	DUN & BRADSTREET CORP	DNB	82	SCHLUMBERGER LTD	SLB
33	EASTMAN KODAK CO	EK	83	SEAGRAM CO LTD	VO
34	ELI LILLY & CO	LLY	84	SOUTHERN CO	SO
35	EMERSON ELECTRIC CO	EMR	85	SOUTHWESTERN BELL CORP	SBC
36	EXXON CORP	XON	86	SYNTEX CORP	SYN
37	FOOD LION INC	FDLNB	87	TEXACO	TX
38	G T E CORP	GTE	88	TEXAS UTILITIES CO	TXU
39	GANNETT CO INC	GCI	89	U S WEST INC	USW
40	GENERAL ELECTRIC CO	GE	90	UNION PACIFIC CORP	UNP
41	GENERAL MILLS	GIS	91	UNITED TECHNOLOGIES CORP	UTX
42	GILLETTE CO	GS	92	UNITED TELECOMMUNICATIONS	UT
43	HEINZ CO (H J)	HNZ	93	UNOCAL CORP	UCL
44	HEWLETT PACKARD CO	HWP	94	UPJOHN CO	UPJ
45	HOME DEPOT INC	HD	95	WAL MART STORES	WMT
46	INTL BUSINESS MACHINES	IBM	96	WARNER LAMBERT CO	WLA
47	INTL PAPER CO	IP	97	WASTE MANAGEMENT INC	WMX
48	J C PENNEY CO	JCP	98	WESTINGHOUSE ELECTRIC	WX
49	JOHNSON & JOHNSON	JNJ	99	WEYERHAEUSER CO	WY
50	K MART CORP	KM	100	XEROX CORP	XRX

The sensitivity analysis is also quite flexible. You can choose the variables you want to alter and the ranges over which they should run. Here is the result:

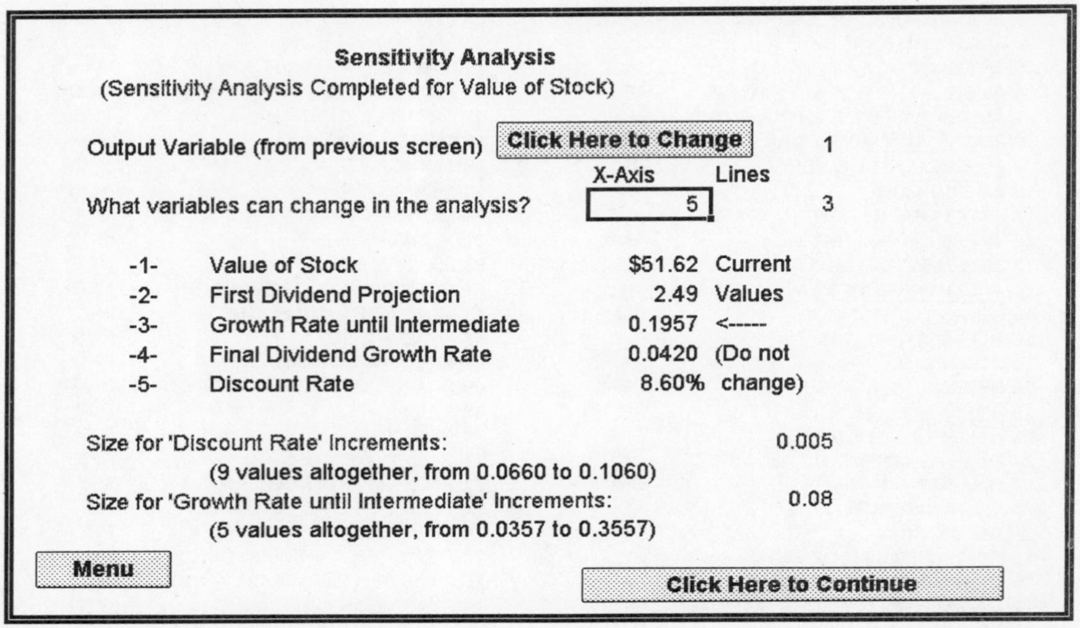
Sensitivity Analysis
(Sensitivity Analysis Completed for Value of Stock)
Output Variable (from previous screen)
Click Here to Change
1
X-Axis
Lines
What variables can change in the analysis?
5
3
-1- Value of Stock $51.62
-2- First Dividend Projection 2.49
-3- Growth Rate until Intermediate 0.1957
-4- Final Dividend Growth Rate 0.0420
-5- Discount Rate 8.60%
Current Values <----- (Do not change)
Size for 'Discount Rate' Increments: 0.005
(9 values altogether, from 0.0660 to 0.1060)
Size for 'Growth Rate until Intermediate' Increments: 0.08
(5 values altogether, from 0.0357 to 0.3557)
Menu
Click Here to Continue

In our case, we are not sure of the discount rate or the final dividend growth rate. The discount rate will run along the X-axis of the graph we produce, and the effect of different growth rates will be shown by lines on the graph. The increments for the discount rate are 0.005 and the increments for the growth rate are 0.08. Note that when you change the increments, the text underneath the statement to the left alters in response to your change. If these ranges are correct, we may proceed.

Click the **Click Here to Continue** button to automatically recalculate the sensitivity analysis table. The table is shown on the following page.

Sensitivity Analysis

(Sensitivity Analysis Completed for Value of Stock)

Growth Rate until Intermediate

	3.57%	11.57%	19.57%	27.57%	35.57%
6.60%	101.81	126.10	154.08	186.01	222.16
7.10%	84.27	104.18	127.11	153.27	182.87
7.60%	71.89	88.71	108.08	130.16	155.15
8.10%	62.68	77.21	93.93	112.99	134.55
8.60%	55.57	68.33	83.00	99.73	118.64
9.10%	49.90	61.26	74.31	89.18	105.99
9.60%	45.29	55.50	67.23	80.59	95.68
10.10%	41.46	50.71	61.35	73.45	87.13
10.60%	38.22	46.68	56.39	67.44	79.93

Discount Rate

Menu | Click Here for Graph | Click Here to Continue

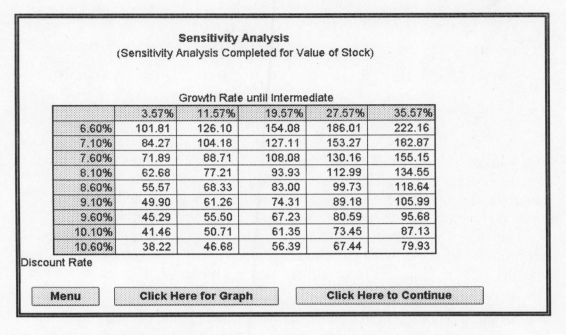

Click the **Click Here for Graph** to view the following visual presentation.

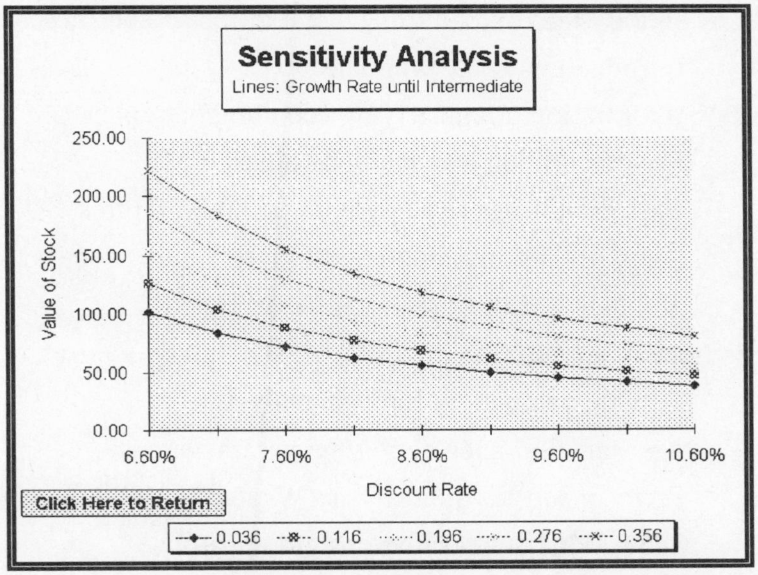
Sensitivity Analysis
Lines: Growth Rate until Intermediate
250.00
200.00
150.00
100.00
50.00
0.00
Value of Stock
6.60%
7.60%
8.60%
9.60%
10.60%
Discount Rate
Click Here to Return
0.036
0.116
0.196
0.276
0.356

Test your understanding of this worksheet by completing the *Problems to Accompany The Two-Dividend Growth Model*, which appears later in this manual.

Worksheet 9
Futures Pricing
Specific Instructions and a Numerical Example

FUTURES.XLS

This worksheet is designed to help the student understand futures pricing using the cost-of-carry relationships. The worksheet offers pricing capabilities, and can calculate implied values of any of the input variables: the underlying spot price, the interest rate, the convenience yield, the cost of carry, and the dividend rate. The student can establish a position, forecast profits and losses, perform simulations of contract values, and finally analyze several scenarios with the built-in "What-if?" capabilities. This is a powerful, all-purpose futures pricing worksheet.

The organization of the worksheet is similar to others in the package:

Menu: Click this button to return to the *Futures Pricing Menu* screen

Use the buttons on the *Menu* screen to navigate to the screens described below:

Intro: Introduction to the worksheet

Background: Information on underlying economic variables

Pricing: Futures pricing and implied values

Holdings: User establishes strategy with cash and futures

Forecast: Show profits and losses for a given future scenario

Simulation: Simulate a path of cash and futures prices

Risk-Analysis Items:

Data: Provide parameters for risk analysis

Help: Assistance in interpreting the parameters

Sensitivity: Perform sensitivity analysis (What-if?)

Graph: Show What-if? calculations graphically

Print: Print your results

Quit: Return to *The Innovative Investor* menu

In this worksheet almost every screen has a descriptive backup screen that can be accessed by clicking the **Click Here for Help** buttons. Each help screen has a **Return** button.

Here are the two introductory screens.

Futures Pricing

This spreadsheet values futures contracts under the cost-of-carry approach. The interest rate, carrying cost on the underlying commodity, and the dividend rate on the underlying commodity are assumed to be constant, continuous, and proportional to the price level.

For the sake of approximation, we allow the cost-of-carry variables to change, but caution the user that the theoretical pricing model assumes they remain constant. Any pricing results here are intended for educational uses only, and should not be construed as investment advice!

The spreadsheet was designed to help you learn about futures and futures pricing.

Click Here to Continue

Menu

Futures Pricing Spreadsheet : Introduction (Part 2)

You may perform the following analyses with this spreadsheet:

- Futures pricing
- Implied values from futures prices
- Position evaluation: cash and futures
- Profit/Loss analysis: changes in the spot price and cost-of-carry assumptions
- Simulation of cash and futures price paths
- Tabular and graphical "What-if?" analysis

The program assumes that the cost-of-carry variables are constant and that the underlying spot commodity follows a proportional random walk.

Change highlighted values only.

Click Here to Continue

Menu

Next, there is some background information users must enter before proceeding. The worksheet can handle futures contracts on a single cash commodity — but only up to three expiration dates in the futures. For the rest of the analysis, the cost-of-carry relationship is assumed to hold at all times.

Futures Pricing Spreadsheet: Background Information

Spot Commodity Name:	corn	(lower case)
(The following 2 items are not required for futures pricing)		
Average annual growth rate:	0.00%	
Volatility of annual growth rate:	25.00%	
Unit multiplier:	40,000	
Futures contract maturity dates:		
Contract #1:	0.25	years
Contract #2:	0.50	years
Contract #3:	0.75	years

Click Here for Help   Click Here to Continue

Menu

This is the *Help* screen for *Background Information.*

Futures Pricing Spreadsheet: Background Information

The name of the spot commodity is required for display purposes, and does not affect any calculations.

The average growth rate and volatility are used in simulations, but are not required for the pricing of the futures contracts.

The effective margin requirement is assumed here to be zero, since futures traders may often post interest-bearing securities as margin. If this is not the case, traders may price the effect of margins into futures prices.

The multiplier tells the spreadsheet that, for example, you will quote the per bushel price of corn, but the contract covers M bushels, where M is the multiplier.

You may evaluate up to three different futures contracts.

The next step is to price the futures contracts, or to determine implied parameter values from market futures prices. The user selects one of the three contracts for analysis, and indicates which variable (1..5) is unknown. The program takes the data assumptions in the DATA column, and shows the single calculation in the

RESULT column. In the example below, the datum $323.216 in the data column is ignored.

Pricing and Implied Values

Select contract for implied value calculations: 2

	Contract #1:	0.25	years	
--->	Contract #2:	0.50	years	<----
	Contract #3:	0.75	years	

Select a variable to solve for: 5

			DATA	RESULT	
	1	Price of corn	$0.500	-----	
	2	Interest rate	8.00%	-----	
	3	Cost of carrying corn	2.00%	-----	
	4	Dividend payment rate	1.00%	-----	
--->	5	Futures price	$0.523	$0.523	<----

Click Here for Help

Click Here to Copy RESULT to DATA

Click Here to Continue

Menu

Pricing and Implied Values Interpretation and Help

Select any of the three futures contracts you specified above for analysis. There are five variables in the futures pricing function; you may provide any four while the program finds the missing fifth.

Steps:
1. Select the missing variable number.
2. Provide the missing data in the DATA column.
3. See your calculation in the RESULT column.

Next, the user may establish a position in the cash contract and the three futures contracts.

In this case, we are long two cash contracts (80,000 bushels of corn) and short one futures contract with maturity 0.5 years. Once again, there is further help interpreting your results.

Position Entry

Enter your position below:

		Shadow Value	Value in Position
Units of corn:	2	$0.500	$1.000
Units of contract #1:	0	$0.511	$0.000
Units of contract #2:	-1	$0.523	($0.523)
Units of contract #3:	0	$0.535	$0.000

Cash value of position	$40,000.00
Shadow value of position	$19,079.44

Click Here for Help

Click Here to Continue

Menu

Position Entry

Positive numbers indicate long positions.
Negative numbers indicate short positions.
Fractional positions are allowed.

The SHADOW VALUE shows the value of the position as if the futures contracts were assets, like stocks. It is not a realistic representation of the cash value of the position; however, changes in the shadow value are exactly identical to changes in the cash value.

The CASH value is the cost of establishing the position assuming zero effective futures margin.

Now we can complete a mini-scenario analysis. In this case, I wish to look at what will happen to my position 36 days in the future (0.10 years) if the price of corn drops $0.10, interest rates go up 2%, the carrying cost doesn't change, and the dividend yield (i.e., convenience yield) decreases by 1%. The calculations show that I can expect to lose about $4,446.21. The calculations are not exact because the changes we specified might have taken place any time during the 36 day period.

Profit/Loss Forecast

Forecast ahead (years) 0.10 (Must be less than 0.25)

FORECAST CHANGES ONLY:	Current	--> Change	Forecasted
Price of corn:*	$0.500	($0.100)	$0.400
Interest rate:	8.00%	2.00%	10.00%
Carrying cost:	2.00%	0.00%	2.00%
Dividend rate:	1.00%	-1.00%	0.00%

*(The chance that corn exceeds 0.400 in 0.10 years is 100%)

Position profit/loss		(4,068.83)	
Interest recd/paid	(402.01)	-	(288.60)
Carrying costs	(80.08)	-	(64.06)
Dividends received	0.00	-	39.98
Total profit/loss	(4,550.91)	-	(4,381.51)
Average total profit/loss		(4,466.21)	

Click Here for Help | Click Here to Continue

Menu

Profit/Loss Forecast Interpretations

This screen asks you to choose a planning horizon, and hypothetically allow the underlying spot price and other assumptions to change.

Put the CHANGES in the values only; the current values and forecasted values are provided for your reference.

The probability is based on the average growth and volatility you supplied.

POSITION PROFIT/LOSS shows your profit or loss on the on the cash/futures position if the forecast materializes. The next three rows show a summary of the other possible gains and losses. The AVERAGE TOTAL PROFIT/LOSS takes the simple average of the minimum and maximum profit/loss.

The following simulation section is optional. We may choose to plot two contract values over some period of time. Choose the variable numbers and the time horizon. Then click the **Activate** button to load the simulator. The worksheet will graph a simulation for you, as seen on the next page. **Simulate** gives you a different simulation each time it is clicked. **Deactivate** unloads the simulator. In general, you will allow the rest of the program to run more quickly if you deactivate the simulator.

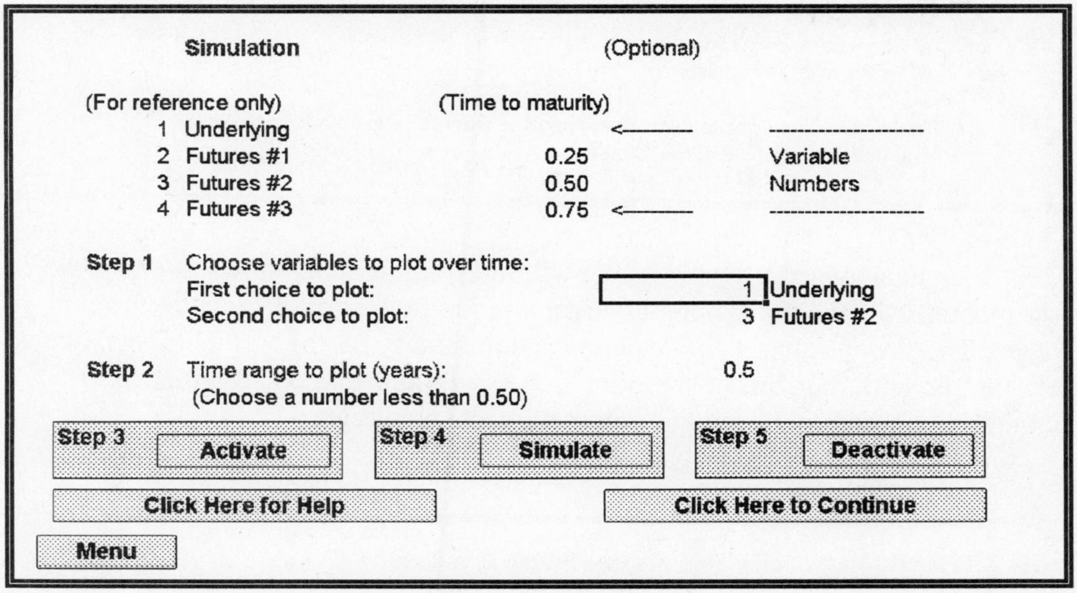
Simulation
(Optional)
(For reference only)
(Time to maturity)
1 Underlying
2 Futures #1 0.25
3 Futures #2 0.50
4 Futures #3 0.75
Variable Numbers
Step 1 Choose variables to plot over time:
First choice to plot: 1 Underlying
Second choice to plot: 3 Futures #2
Step 2 Time range to plot (years): 0.5
(Choose a number less than 0.50)
Step 3 Activate
Step 4 Simulate
Step 5 Deactivate
Click Here for Help
Click Here to Continue
Menu

Simulation HELP

This section is optional. There are five steps involved.

You may plot a simulated sequence of any two contracts. The contracts may be the cash commodity or any futures you have previously specified. All costs of carry are assumed constant.

Steps:
1. Indicate which series to plot.
2. Indicate the time horizon.
3. Activate the simulator.
4. Simulate as many times as you like.
5. Deactivate the simulator.

The simulator is activated and deactivated in order to save computation time on the rest of the spreadsheet.

Click Here to Return

This is an example of a graph drawn with the simulator. It shows over the next six months how the underlying contract and the futures might relate to each other. The lower value is the underlying commodity (corn) and the upper line is the futures with (currently) six months to expiration. Of course, after six months, the prices between these two contracts converge:

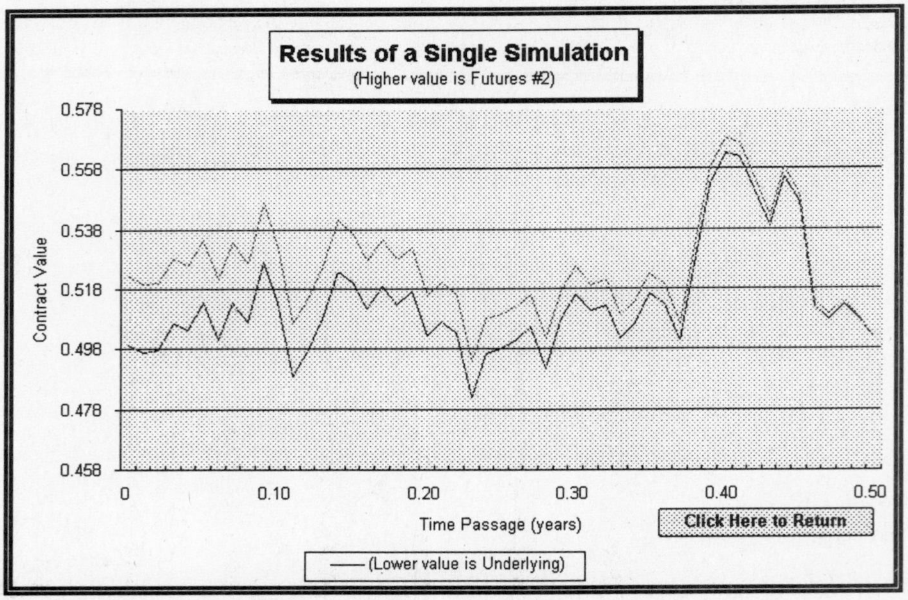
Results of a Single Simulation
(Higher value is Futures #2)
Contract Value
0.578
0.558
0.538
0.518
0.498
0.478
0.458
0
0.10
0.20
0.30
0.40
0.50
Time Passage (years)
Click Here to Return
(Lower value is Underlying)

The risk analysis features of the program come in four screens: *Data, Help, Sensitivity* and *Graph*. The *Data* section appears below. It asks the question, “How should the risk analysis appear?” You may determine which variable to change (except the spot price), the range of the variables to consider, and which variable to display. **IMPORTANT NOTE:** Make sure your forecast screen has the right values in place — this analysis assumes that your prior scenario data is correct.

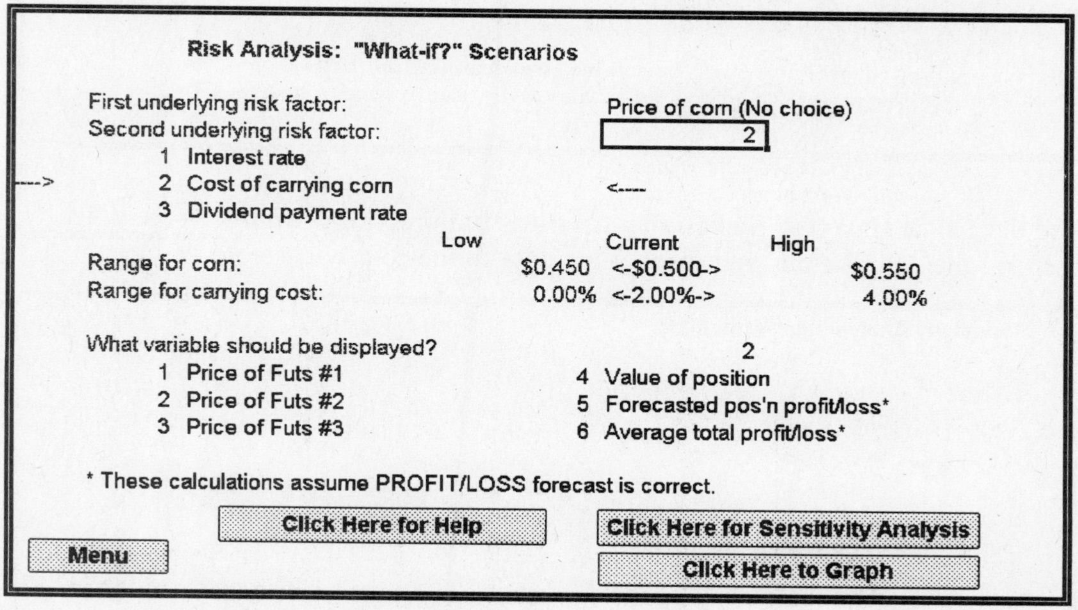
Risk Analysis: "What-if?" Scenarios
First underlying risk factor:
Price of corn (No choice)
Second underlying risk factor:
2
1 Interest rate
---> 2 Cost of carrying corn <----
3 Dividend payment rate
Low
Current
High
Range for corn: $0.450 <-$0.500-> $0.550
Range for carrying cost: 0.00% <-2.00%-> 4.00%
What variable should be displayed?
2
1 Price of Futs #1
2 Price of Futs #2
3 Price of Futs #3
4 Value of position
5 Forecasted pos'n profit/loss*
6 Average total profit/loss*
* These calculations assume PROFIT/LOSS forecast is correct.
Click Here for Help
Click Here for Sensitivity Analysis
Menu
Click Here to Graph

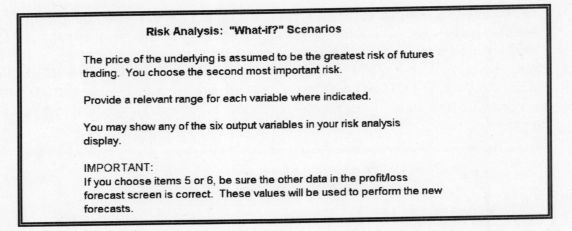

Risk Analysis: "What-if?" Scenarios

The price of the underlying is assumed to be the greatest risk of futures trading. You choose the second most important risk.

Provide a relevant range for each variable where indicated.

You may show any of the six output variables in your risk analysis display.

IMPORTANT:
If you choose items 5 or 6, be sure the other data in the profit/loss forecast screen is correct. These values will be used to perform the new forecasts.

Use the **Click Here for Sensitivity Analysis** button on the *What-if?* screen to perform the calculations and display the data in the following table.

Sensitivity Analysis performed for: Price of Futs #2

		Cost of carrying corn				
		0.00%	1.00%	2.00%	3.00%	4.00%
Price of corn	$0.450	0.473	0.475	0.478	0.480	0.483
	$0.460	0.484	0.486	0.488	0.491	0.493
	$0.470	0.494	0.497	0.499	0.502	0.504
	$0.480	0.505	0.507	0.510	0.512	0.515
	$0.490	0.515	0.518	0.520	0.523	0.526
	$0.500	0.526	0.528	0.531	0.534	0.536
	$0.510	0.536	0.539	0.542	0.544	0.547
	$0.520	0.547	0.549	0.552	0.555	0.558
	$0.530	0.557	0.560	0.563	0.566	0.568
	$0.540	0.568	0.571	0.573	0.576	0.579
	$0.550	0.578	0.581	0.584	0.587	0.590

Menu **Click Here to Return**

You can view this data in chart form by returning to the *What-if?* screen and using the **Click Here to Graph** button.

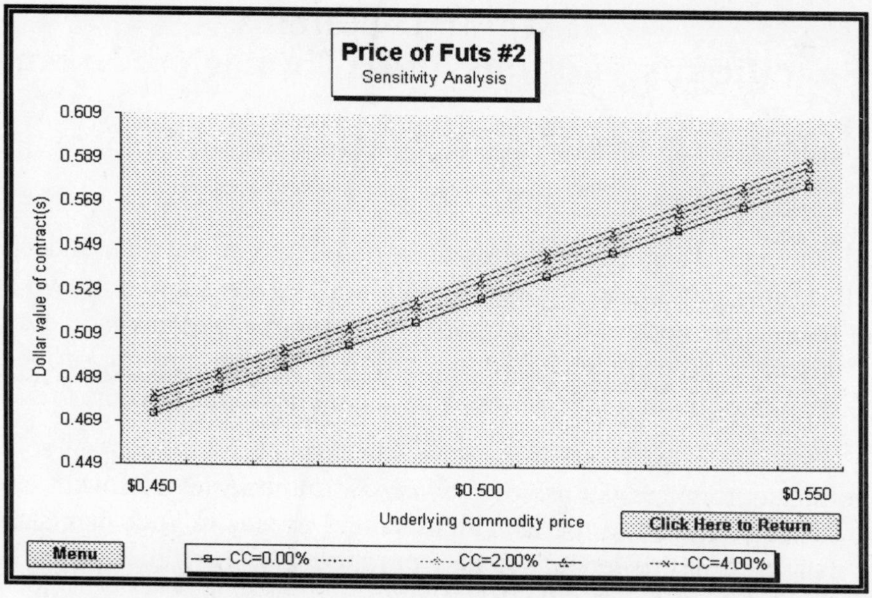
Price of Futs #2
Sensitivity Analysis
0.609
0.589
0.569
0.549
0.529
0.509
0.489
0.469
0.449
Dollar value of contract(s)
$0.450
$0.500
$0.550
Underlying commodity price
Click Here to Return
Menu
CC=0.00%
CC=2.00%
CC=4.00%

Overall, the futures pricing and risk management worksheet can be used in many ways to solve a great variety of problems. Test your understanding of this worksheet by completing the *Problems to Accompany Futures Pricing*, which appears later in this manual.

Worksheet 10
Hedging Dynamics
Specific Instructions and a Numerical Example

HEDGE.XLS

HEDGE intends to serve two purposes. We assume you have an underlying series of returns relating to a portfolio you hold. At the same time, you may wish to form cross-hedges for that portfolio, either to take advantage of market timing beliefs, or to truly hedge your position. The first purpose of the program is to determine optimal hedge ratios. The second is to allow you to set up a competing hedge for your underlying position.

This worksheet requires the use of *Crunch*. Both the series you want to hedge and the series you want to use as hedges should appear in your data set. The sample data used in this manual came from the *pdata.xls* file. Use the **Prepare CRUNCH Data** and **Load CRUNCH Data** buttons as needed to import your series of returns. If your data were in the form of gross or net returns, the latest price was assumed to be $1. You may wish to change this figure later in the program.

The four screens displayed below provide useful background information for using the Hedge worksheet.

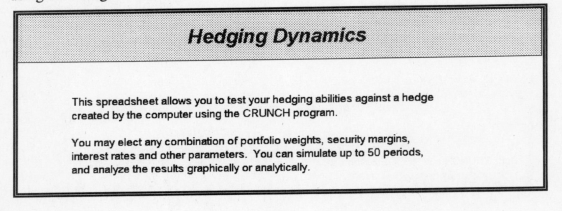

Hedging Dynamics

This spreadsheet allows you to test your hedging abilities against a hedge created by the computer using the CRUNCH program.

You may elect any combination of portfolio weights, security margins, interest rates and other parameters. You can simulate up to 50 periods, and analyze the results graphically or analytically.

HEDGE

The purpose of this spreadsheet is twofold. Imagine that you hold a position in any portfolio, and that you have tracked the returns on this portfolio through time. Sometimes, you want to hedge your portfolio against variation in its returns; you may be a hedger in the usual sense of an agricultural producer, or you may wish to transform a stock position into a bond position without incurring overwhelming transaction costs.

Therefore, you choose up to 10 other securities or futures contracts you might use to create a minimum variance hedge for your portfolio. Naturally, you will have to track the returns of each of these hedge candidates over the same time period as your hedged portfolio, and assume that past data can be used to extrapolate into the future. A program called CRUNCH then can transform your data into the set of statistics this spreadsheet needs.

The first thing this spreadsheet calculates for you is the set of optimal hedge ratios. You may stop here if you like; these data are critical for establishing a hedge position.

Alternatively, you might wish to invent hedge ratios of your own, and see whether you can "beat the computer" at the hedging game. You can specify the margin required for each contract. The computer will simulate several periods using historical returns, volatilities, and correlations --- period by period, you can see how well your hedge has performed against the optimal hedge. You also have the choice of rebalancing terms; with constant hedge ratios, you may allow both the computer and yourself to rebalance every period, or you may choose precommitment to a single hedge creation.

The Data screen allows you to rerun CRUNCH and import different data sets.
The Hedge screen allows you to establish your own position and state the margin requirements; i.e., what percentage of the value of each security must be posted as margin.

The Simulate screen actually runs the simulation for you; the Graph and Results buttons allow you to compare your performance in graphical or tabular form against the hedged contract.

Overall, we want to ask the question, "How well did the optimal hedge perform over a simulated future scenario? And how did our portfolio perform?"

TECHNICAL NOTE:

Both CRUNCH and HEDGE assume that the return data are generated by joint normal processes, with constant parameters equal to those of the chosen historical period. In its simplest form, HEDGE can be used to simulate values of jointly normally distributed variables through time.

The *Data* screen looks exactly like *The Efficient Portfolio Frontier*. You can use this screen to run *Crunch* to select different sets of underlying return series from which expected returns, correlations, names and last prices are imported. Unlike *The Efficient Portfolio Frontier* you should *not* change the data manually. *Crunch* provides additional statistical calculations for this sheet that would not match your manually entered data and would result in inaccurate output.

BACKGROUND DATA

Please use the Prepare CRUNCH Data and Load CRUNCH Data buttons to provide the names, expected returns and standard deviations of up to 10 securities.

Data CRUNCH Utility

Prepare CRUNCH Data

Load CRUNCH Data

The correlation matrix will also be automatically provided.

NOTES:
No riskless assets allowed.
Start at #1.

Click Here to Clear Data

Menu

No.	Name	Exp Ret	Std Dev	Last Price
1	T	9.7%	15.0%	1.00
2	BS	4.7%	27.7%	1.00
3	BA	21.6%	37.6%	1.00
4	CHU	12.5%	23.8%	1.00
5	KO	14.7%	20.9%	1.00
6	DD	5.9%	20.9%	1.00
7	EK	9.2%	21.3%	1.00
8	XON	12.7%	17.5%	1.00
9	GE	9.1%	21.9%	1.00
10	GM	9.8%	20.0%	1.00

Number of Securities 10

Click Here to Continue

Use the *Hedge* screen to establish the hedge parameters. Our underlying portfolio name is VWCRSP; yours may be different. We assume you are fully invested in 2 units VWCRSP supplemented with $1,000 cash.

If the type of your underlying data is net returns or gross returns the amount in *Last Value of VWCRSP* (security you want to hedge) will be $1. In this situation you should enter the actual last value of the security as we have done in the example. If the type of your underlying data is price the Last Value cell will already contain the correct amount.

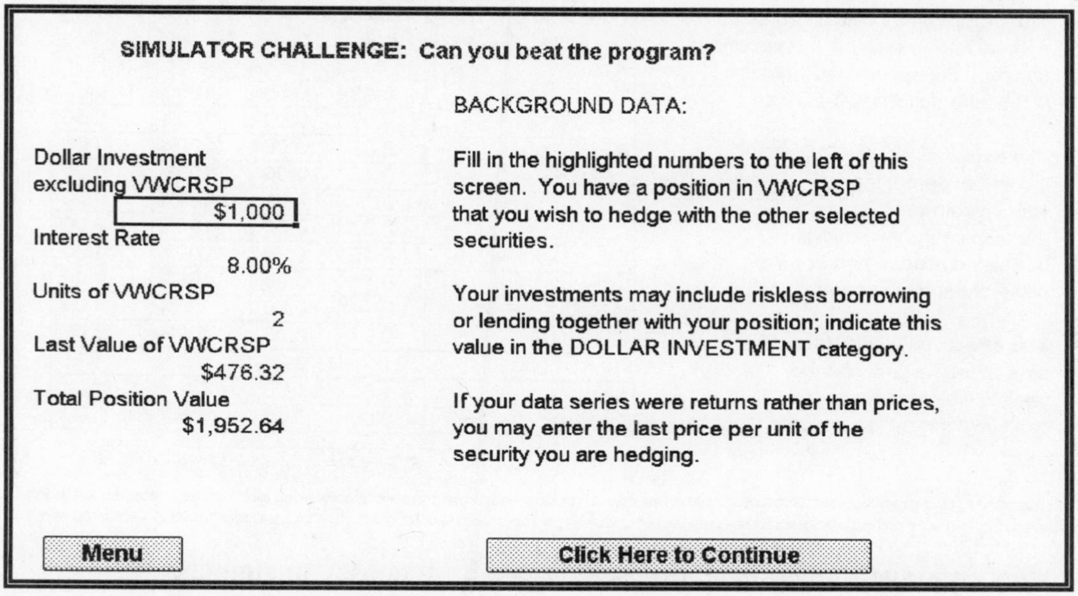
SIMULATOR CHALLENGE: Can you beat the program?
BACKGROUND DATA:
Dollar Investment excluding VWCRSP
$1,000
Interest Rate
8.00%
Units of VWCRSP
2
Last Value of VWCRSP
$476.32
Total Position Value
$1,952.64
Fill in the highlighted numbers to the left of this screen. You have a position in VWCRSP that you wish to hedge with the other selected securities.
Your investments may include riskless borrowing or lending together with your position; indicate this value in the DOLLAR INVESTMENT category.
If your data series were returns rather than prices, you may enter the last price per unit of the security you are hedging.
Menu
Click Here to Continue

The optimal hedge ratios appear in the Prog column of the next screen. At this point, the first objective has been achieved. You can finish by writing down the displayed portfolio weights or you can try your hand at improving on the computer-generated ratios. In the example, we have chosen a cheaper cross-hedge (cheaper in transaction costs) of a 50/50 position in T and BS. Let's see how we do.

Program and Competing Portfolio Weights

The program has calculated its optimal hedge ratios in the second column. Place your hedge ratios in the third column.

The margin figure represents the actual percentage of your investment that was made in cash. Any margin borrowing is assumed to take place at the riskless rate.

The effective weights demonstrate that margins change relative weights when the cash investment is the same.

Security	Per-Unit Wts Prog	Per-Unit Wts Yours	Margin	Effective Wts
T	0.12	0.50	100%	0.50
BS	0.09	0.50	100%	0.50
BA	0.07	0.00	100%	0.00
CHU	0.12	0.00	100%	0.00
KO	0.12	0.00	100%	0.00
DD	0.07	0.00	100%	0.00
EK	0.10	0.00	100%	0.00
XON	0.11	0.00	100%	0.00
GE	0.14	0.00	100%	0.00
GM	0.07	0.00	100%	0.00
Sum	1.00	1.00		1.00
Riskless	0.00	0.00		0.00

Click Here to Continue

As we continue to the *Simulation* screen, we have chosen to simulate 10 periods, and to rebalance the portfolio every period. Changing values change relative weights, so the optimal hedge portfolio must readjust. The simulation is carried out assuming that returns are jointly lognormally distributed, with parameters equal to their historical values. Click the **Activate Simulator** to run the simulation for the specified number of periods.

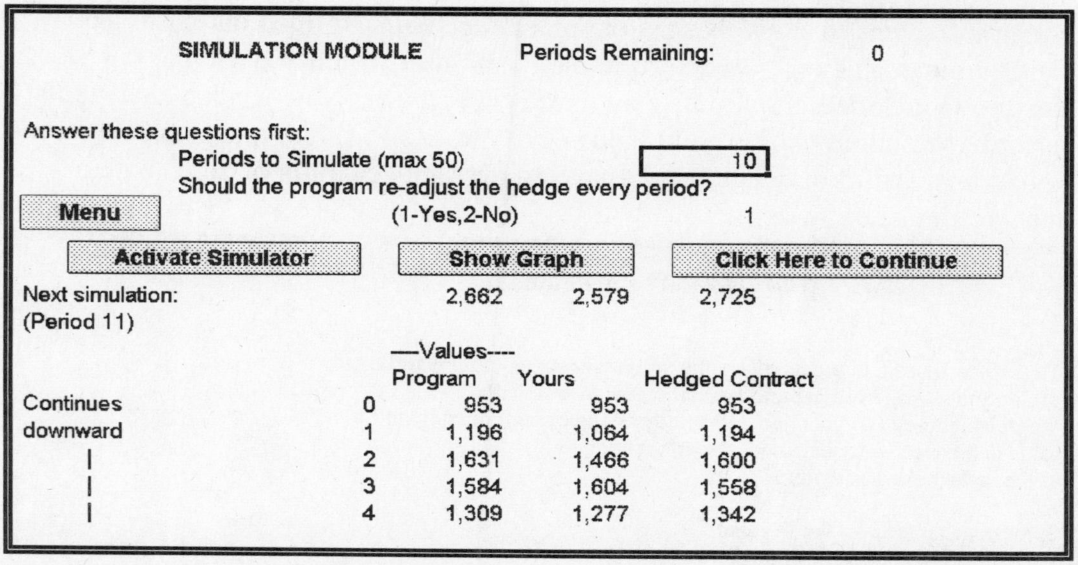
SIMULATION MODULE Periods Remaining: 0

Answer these questions first:
Periods to Simulate (max 50) 10
Should the program re-adjust the hedge every period?
(1-Yes,2-No) 1

Menu

Activate Simulator | Show Graph | Click Here to Continue

Next simulation: 2,662 2,579 2,725
(Period 11)

		----Values----		
		Program	Yours	Hedged Contract
Continues	0	953	953	953
downward	1	1,196	1,064	1,194
|	2	1,631	1,466	1,600
|	3	1,584	1,604	1,558
|	4	1,309	1,277	1,342

These numbers show what happened to VWCRSP, to the optimal hedge portfolio (Program) and our competing hedge portfolio (Yours). It's hard to digest this data all at once, so click the **Show Graph** button see the data in chart form.

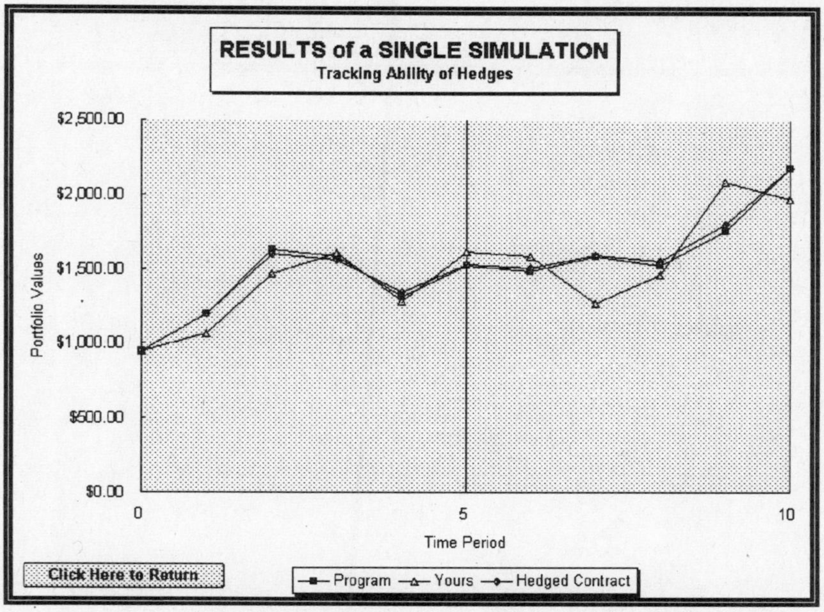
RESULTS of a SINGLE SIMULATION
Tracking Ability of Hedges
$2,500.00
$2,000.00
$1,500.00
$1,000.00
$500.00
$0.00
Portfolio Values
0
5
10
Time Period
Click Here to Return
Program
Yours
Hedged Contract

The graph seems to show that the optimal hedge outperformed our own. To confirm our suspicions, we return to the *Simulation* screen and use the **Click Here to Continue** button to display the *Results* screen. Now we can analyze the performance in terms of present value of deviations in value, and standard deviations. The ideal hedge would have an average deviation of zero, with a standard deviation of zero.

SIMULATION SUMMARY and RESULTS

To provide a basis for comparison, the spreadsheet has determined profits and losses in each period as a result of following the program strategy and your hedging strategy. The per period present value of the loss was calculated. A perfect hedge will have all these values equal to zero.

Summary Statistics for the Present Value of Profit/Loss per Period (discounted at expected growth rate of VWCRSP	Program Results	Your Results
Mean	0.15	10.52
Standard Deviation	18.04	132.72
Standard Deviation of Mean Estimate	5.71	41.97

Menu | Click Here to Continue

The final screen displays the actual profit/loss by period. The left side of this screen matches present value of deviations between the competing hedges, while the right side matches returns.

Profit/Loss by Period

Click Here to Restart

Menu

Discounted* Profits/Losses (at rate of hedged contract)

Continues downward

Period	Program	Your		----Returns----- Program	Your	VWCRSP
0	0.00	0.00	|	#N/A	#N/A	#N/A
1	(1.84)	118.79	|	25.5%	11.7%	25.3%
2	(23.48)	3.75	|	36.4%	37.8%	34.1%
3	3.59	(137.12)	|	-2.9%	9.4%	-2.6%
4	40.80	76.86	|	-17.3%	-20.4%	-13.9%
5	(15.54)	(91.54)	|	16.3%	26.0%	14.1%
6	9.54	(1.26)	|	-2.8%	-1.5%	-1.8%
7	(9.12)	219.13	|	7.1%	-20.4%	5.8%
8	11.31	(117.31)	|	-4.2%	15.7%	-2.7%
9	6.98	(167.02)	|	15.1%	42.5%	15.8%
10	(20.76)	200.93	|	24.6%	-5.6%	21.1%
11	0.00	0.00	|	0.0%	0.0%	0.0%
12	0.00	0.00	|	0.0%	0.0%	0.0%
13	0.00	0.00	|	0.0%	0.0%	0.0%
14	0.00	0.00	|	0.0%	0.0%	0.0%

Test your understanding of this worksheet by completing the *Problems to Accompany Hedging Dynamics*, which appears later in this manual.

Worksheet 11
Options Risk Analysis
Specific Instructions and a Numerical Example

OPTRISK.XLS

This worksheet is probably the most advanced and difficult of all the worksheets in *The Innovative Investor*. It enables you to study a multi-legged option position with several complicating factors that *Quick European Option Pricing* does not have. For example, it admits different reporting standards using actual dates, allows futures contracts and commissions to enter the analysis, and calculates holding period returns for these complex positions. Two types of analysis are seen here: the first, *scenario analysis*, allows you to specify the conditions of the market some time in the future and see what happens to your position value and risk sensitivities. The second, *risk analysis*, looks at a range of possible values for different risk variables under consideration. This section will walk you through a sample calculation. You may wish to enter the same data and follow along with your computer. The Introduction contains two screens of instructions.

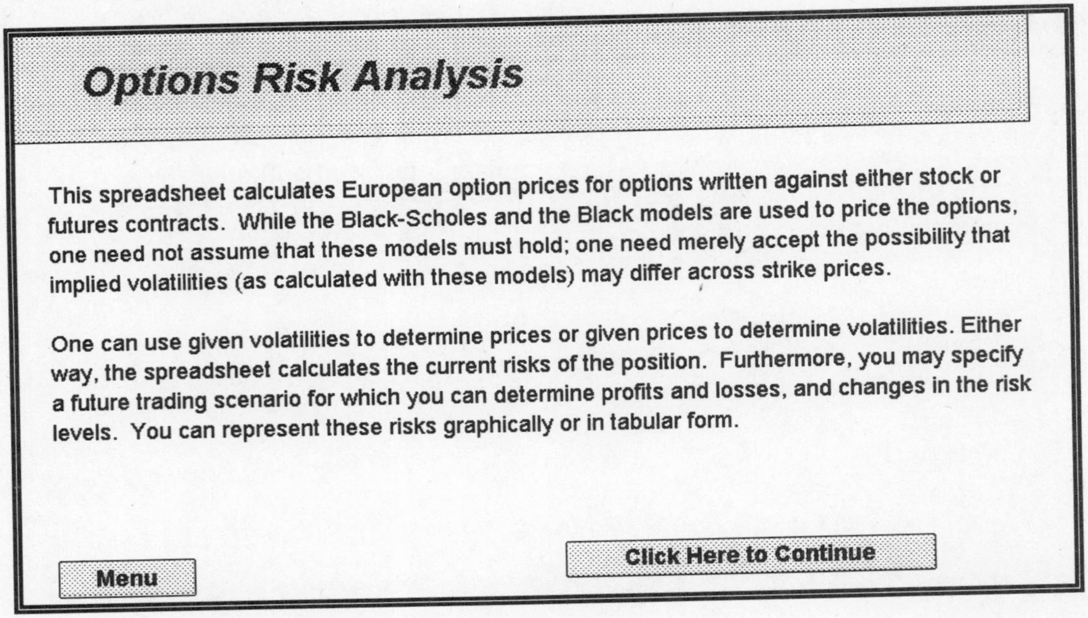
Options Risk Analysis
This spreadsheet calculates European option prices for options written against either stock or futures contracts. While the Black-Scholes and the Black models are used to price the options, one need not assume that these models must hold; one need merely accept the possibility that implied volatilities (as calculated with these models) may differ across strike prices.
One can use given volatilities to determine prices or given prices to determine volatilities. Either way, the spreadsheet calculates the current risks of the position. Furthermore, you may specify a future trading scenario for which you can determine profits and losses, and changes in the risk levels. You can represent these risks graphically or in tabular form.
Menu
Click Here to Continue

The model for volatility used in this spreadsheet can be explained as follows: We assume that the Black or Black-Scholes model is correct for each option, and calculate an implied volatility. This procedure generally gives a different implied volatility for each exercise price. When the spreadsheet refers to a 1% increase in volatility across the board, this means that the implied volatilities are increased by 1% for each option, and the price of each option is recalculated using the higher volatility and the appropriate option-pricing formula.

To use the spreadsheet, you must supply the background data first. You can then perform sensitivity and risk analyses related to your options position. Click the Menu button to view the risk options at any time.

Click Here to Continue

Menu

This program allows you to trade options on stock futures. The standard multipliers for stock are 100; you trade round lots of 100 stocks and lots of 100 options associated with them. For futures, multipliers will vary. Note that if you choose options on futures, even the *instructions* will change! Therefore, it is important to read and answer questions one line at a time.

The rate of return shortfall indicates a continuous dividend yield for stock, or a convenience yield for futures.

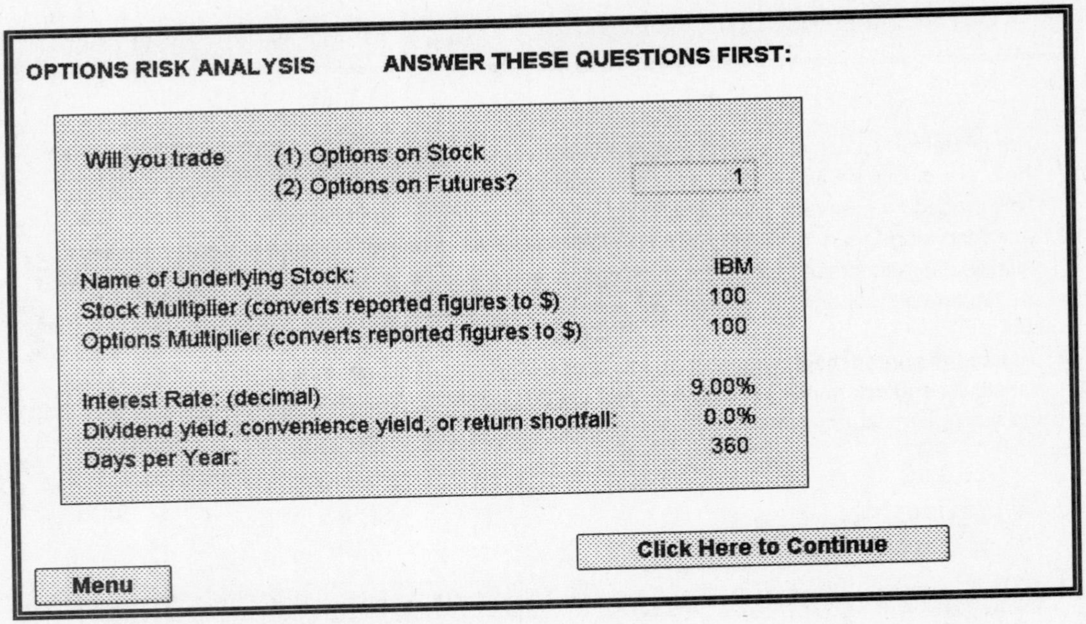

OPTIONS RISK ANALYSIS   ANSWER THESE QUESTIONS FIRST:

Will you trade   (1) Options on Stock
(2) Options on Futures?   1

Name of Underlying Stock:	IBM
Stock Multiplier (converts reported figures to $)	100
Options Multiplier (converts reported figures to $)	100
Interest Rate: (decimal)	9.00%
Dividend yield, convenience yield, or return shortfall:	0.0%
Days per Year:	360

Menu   Click Here to Continue

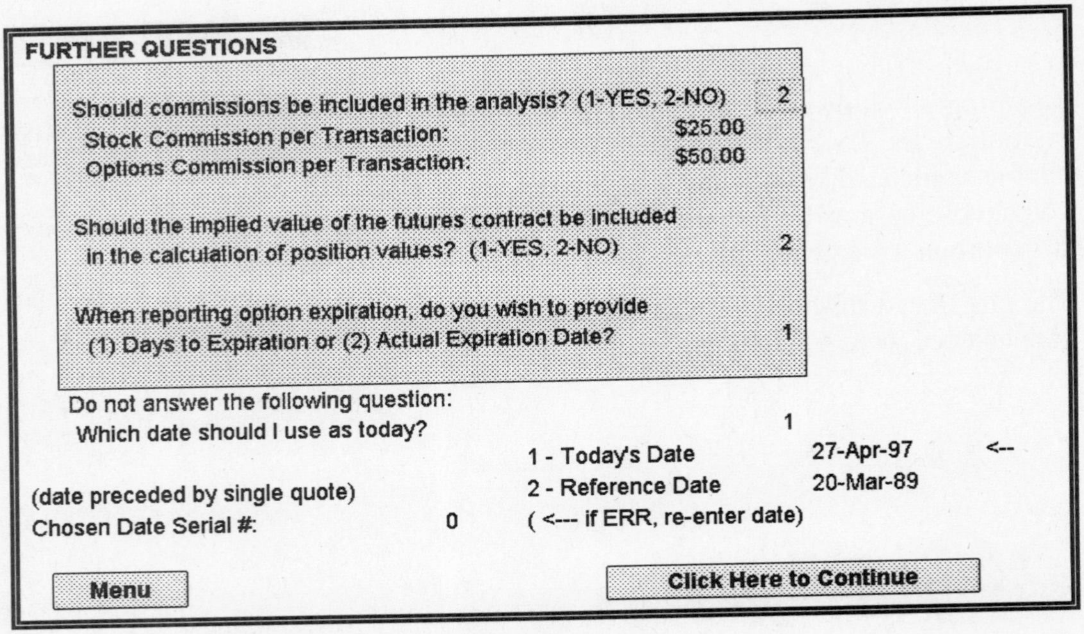

FURTHER QUESTIONS

Should commissions be included in the analysis? (1-YES, 2-NO)	2
Stock Commission per Transaction:	$25.00
Options Commission per Transaction:	$50.00
Should the implied value of the futures contract be included in the calculation of position values? (1-YES, 2-NO)	2
When reporting option expiration, do you wish to provide (1) Days to Expiration or (2) Actual Expiration Date?	1

Do not answer the following question:
Which date should I use as today?   1

1 - Today's Date   27-Apr-97   <--
(date preceded by single quote)   2 - Reference Date   20-Mar-89
Chosen Date Serial #:   0   (<--- if ERR, re-enter date)

Menu   Click Here to Continue

You may elect to include commissions or not. Since futures contracts have no value per se, they are generally not included in the tabulation of position values. Nevertheless, for purposes of comparison, you may include the equivalent dollar value when tabulating the position. You may also choose at this point whether you want to count days to expiration, or use newspaper quotes and actual expiration dates. For the latter procedure, we recommend the acquisition of a CBOE (Chicago Board Options Exchange) expiration calendar.

Now it gets tricky. Click the **Click Here to Continue** button to input your data. You will get the following screen. If the input doesn't seem obvious, click the **Click Here for Help** button. The *Data Formatting* screen will appear as shown on the next page. In the sample, the program indicates that you should provide the volatilities, and the program will calculate the option prices (option 2). If you'd like to provide prices and calculate implied volatilities, type **1** in the text box. Click the **Click Here to Calculate** button to perform the required calculations.

OPTION INFORMATION

[Click Here to Calculate]

[Click Here to Clear Data]

Days to Expiration	Not Used	Exer Price	# of Calls	# of Puts	Call Price (Calculated)	Put Price (Calculated)	Call Volat (You Provide)	Put Volat (You Provide)
50	50	100	-3	-2	16.30	0.06	20.0%	20.0%
50	50	110	-2	-3	7.43	1.06	20.0%	20.0%
50	50	120	-5	-4	1.99	5.50	20.0%	20.0%
100	100	100	-3	-2	17.75	0.28	20.0%	20.0%
100	100	110	-2	-3	9.50	1.79	20.0%	20.0%
100	100	120	-5	-4	3.93	5.97	20.0%	20.0%
	0				0.00	0.00	0.0%	0.0%
	0				0.00	0.00	0.0%	0.0%
	0				0.00	0.00	0.0%	0.0%
	0				0.00	0.00	0.0%	0.0%

IBM Stock Price --> 115 1 <- Number of Lots

[Menu] [Click Here for Help] [Click Here to Continue]

DATA FORMATTING INFORMATION

Type of information given: (1-Volatilities, 2-Prices) | 1 |

If you choose 1, the spreadsheet will calculate option prices with the Black or Black-Scholes formula. If you choose 2, the spreadsheet will calculate implied volatilities from given prices.

Each option position takes up exactly one row. Supply the days to expiration, exercise price, no. of options, and volatilities. Your stock position appears in the bottom row. Negative holdings imply short positions. Put volatility equals call unless overwritten.

After you have finished supplying the data, click the Calculate button perform the calculations you want to make. You can also use the Clear Data button to erase the data ranges. To start over or to print your data for future reference, Click the Menu button.

Click Here to Return

Again, instructions will change if you work with futures instead of stocks. If you get in trouble here, the use the **Click Here for Help** button to get more information. It is important that after you input the data, you click the **Click Here to Calculate** button to calculate prices or volatilities.

Now we begin the scenario analysis segment. Click the **Click Here to Continue** button to give the parameters of your forecast. What is your holding period? What do we assume will happen to the market? My sample assumptions follow:

You should indicate what you think the market might do in the upper half of this presentation. The net effect to your position appears in the lower right corner while the changes in the risk parameters appear in the lower left corner. I chose a 10-day forecast with everything staying the same, except that volatility increases 2% across the board. In this example, the note indicates that I should not exceed 50 days; this date marks the expiration of the earliest option. The program will give false results if you exceed the first expiration date in your scenario analysis.

OPTION PRICE AND RISK FORECASTS

ASSUMPTIONS:		Currently:
How many days forward to project?	10	0
By how much does the stock increase?	0	115
By how much does volatility increase?	2.0%	0.0% to 20.0%
How much does the interest rate go up?	0.0%	9.0%
How much does return shortfall go up?	0.0%	0.0%

POSITION SUMMARY:

	Now	Fore-cast
Position Delta:	-5.70	-5.35
Position Vega:	-5.59	-5.24
Position Zeta:	-1.17	-0.95

Total Value Today:	(10,573)
Value Forecast:	(10,673)
Liquidating Comm:	0
Change in Value:	(99)

NOTES: Max 50 days. Use negative numbers for decreases. Volatility in(de)creases across the board. Underlying price assumed unaffected by interest rate changes. Rate of return shortfall includes convenience yield and dividend yield.

Menu | Click Here to Print Forecasts | Click Here to Continue

To see the impact of your assumptions on individual option values, click the **Click Here to Continue** button. The output appears on the following page.

SUMMARY OF INDIVIDUAL FORECASTS

Days to Expiration		Exer Price	# of Calls	# of Puts	Call Price	Put Price	Call Volat	Put Volat
50		100	-3	-2	16.05	0.06	22.0%	22.0%
50		110	-2	-3	7.18	1.09	22.0%	22.0%
50		120	-5	-4	1.85	5.65	22.0%	22.0%
100		100	-3	-2	17.58	0.36	22.0%	22.0%
100		110	-2	-3	9.48	2.03	22.0%	22.0%
100		120	-5	-4	4.02	6.35	22.0%	22.0%
0		0	0	0	0.00	0.00	0.0%	0.0%
0		0	0	0	0.00	0.00	0.0%	0.0%
0		0	0	0	0.00	0.00	0.0%	0.0%
0		0	0	0	0.00	0.00	0.0%	0.0%

Menu | Click Here to Continue

We can also look at our risk measures under the current scenario and the one we have just proposed. To see the current risk measures, click the **Click Here to Continue** button. To see the forecasted risk measures (under our scenario) click the **Click Here to Continue** again. The two outputs appear On the following page.

OPTION COMPARATIVE STATICS RISK ANALYSIS

*Unit move in option per 1 (unit/percent/percent) increase in factor

Days to Expiration	Exer		Underlying ---Deltas--		Volatilities ---Vegas---		Interest Rates ---Zetas---	
			Call	Put	Call	Put	Call	Put
50	100		0.98	-0.02	0.02	0.02	0.13	0.00
50	110		0.79	-0.21	0.12	0.12	0.12	-0.04
50	120		0.36	-0.64	0.16	0.16	0.05	-0.11
100	100		0.95	-0.05	0.07	0.07	0.25	-0.02
100	110		0.76	-0.24	0.19	0.19	0.22	-0.08
100	120		0.45	-0.55	0.24	0.24	0.13	-0.19
0	0		0.00	0.00	0.00	0.00	0.00	0.00
0	0		0.00	0.00	0.00	0.00	0.00	0.00
0	0		0.00	0.00	0.00	0.00	0.00	0.00
0	0		0.00	0.00	0.00	0.00	0.00	0.00

POSITION SUMMARY: -5.70 -5.59 -1.17

Menu

Click Here to Continue

OPTION COMPARATIVE STATICS RISK FORECASTS

*Unit move in option per 1 (unit/percent/percent) increase in factor

Days to Expiration	Exer		Underlying ---Deltas--		Volatilities ---Vegas---		Interest Rates ---Zetas---	
			Call	Put	Call	Put	Call	Put
50	100		0.98	-0.02	0.02	0.02	0.11	0.00
50	110		0.78	-0.22	0.11	0.11	0.09	-0.03
50	120		0.34	-0.66	0.14	0.14	0.04	-0.09
100	100		0.94	-0.06	0.07	0.07	0.23	-0.02
100	110		0.75	-0.25	0.18	0.18	0.19	-0.08
100	120		0.45	-0.55	0.23	0.23	0.12	-0.17
0	0		0.00	0.00	0.00	0.00	0.00	0.00
0	0		0.00	0.00	0.00	0.00	0.00	0.00
0	0		0.00	0.00	0.00	0.00	0.00	0.00
0	0		0.00	0.00	0.00	0.00	0.00	0.00

POSITION SUMMARY: -5.35 -5.24 -0.95

Menu

Click Here to Continue

Using these tables, you can see exactly what will happen to predicted deltas, vagas, and zetas in our 10-day analysis period.

We now proceed to a more general risk-analysis framework.

We allow the underlying and a variable of your choice to move, and analyze their joint impact on the display choice (Forecast in Position Value, etc.) below. The default ranges show you what the range of the underlying and volatility changes are, but you can overwrite these default ranges by changing the numbers in the lower-right corner.

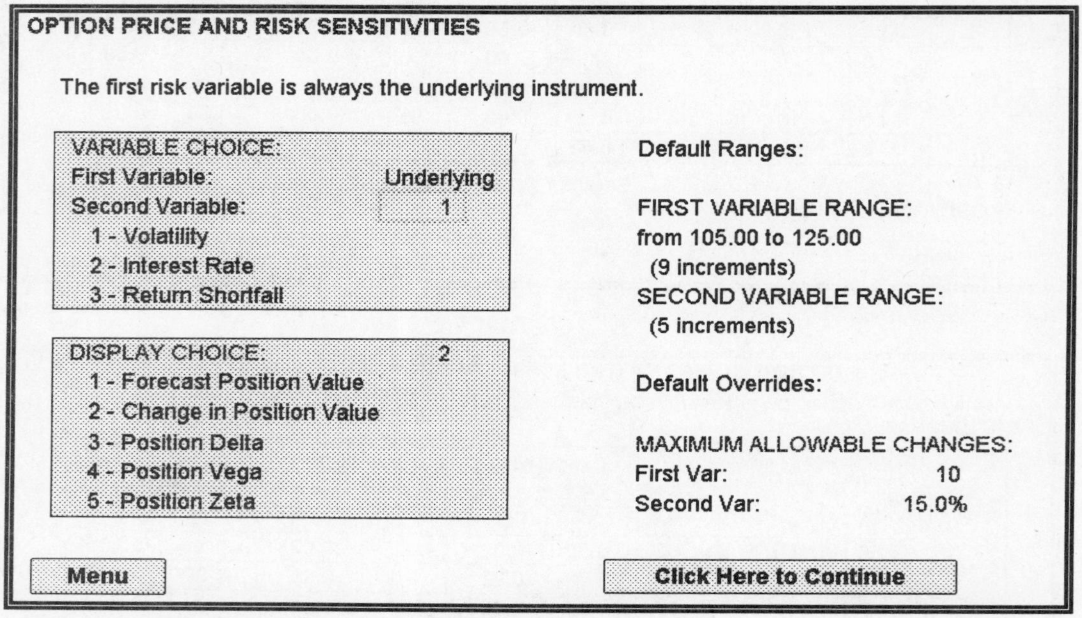
OPTION PRICE AND RISK SENSITIVITIES
The first risk variable is always the underlying instrument.
VARIABLE CHOICE:
First Variable: Underlying
Second Variable: 1
1 - Volatility
2 - Interest Rate
3 - Return Shortfall
DISPLAY CHOICE: 2
1 - Forecast Position Value
2 - Change in Position Value
3 - Position Delta
4 - Position Vega
5 - Position Zeta
Default Ranges:
FIRST VARIABLE RANGE:
from 105.00 to 125.00
(9 increments)
SECOND VARIABLE RANGE:
(5 increments)
Default Overrides:
MAXIMUM ALLOWABLE CHANGES:
First Var: 10
Second Var: 15.0%
Menu
Click Here to Continue

Once you have finished answering these questions, click the **Click to Continue** button to display the *Position Sensitivity Analysis* screen.

POSITION SENSITIVITY ANALYSIS: 10 Days Hence

Change in Position Value by Stock Price and Volatility

Stock Price	Stock Price Change	Changes in Volatility -15.0%	-7.5%	0.0%	7.5%	15.0%
105.00	-10.00	4,591	3,329	711	(2,806)	(6,847)
107.50	-7.50	6,328	4,692	1,808	(1,971)	(6,238)
110.00	-5.00	7,151	5,358	2,228	(1,738)	(6,151)
112.50	-2.50	7,117	5,261	1,938	(2,120)	(6,588)
115.00	0.00	6,614	4,351	930	(3,114)	(7,549)
117.50	2.50	5,291	2,577	(781)	(4,690)	(9,003)
120.00	5.00	2,398	(28)	(3,110)	(6,772)	(10,886)
122.50	7.50	(1,852)	(3,395)	(6,016)	(9,331)	(13,176)
125.00	10.00	(6,538)	(7,340)	(9,414)	(12,324)	(15,853)

Recalculate Table

Change Table Assumptions

Menu

Graph Table

Click Here to Restart

Click the **Recalculate Table** button to perform the risk analysis. These calculations will likely take a long time, so have a cup of coffee.

Use the **Change Table Assumptions** button to return to the previous *Option Price and Risk Sensitivities* screen to select different displays and variables.

The **Graph Table** button displays a visual representation of the *Position Sensitivity Analysis* screen.

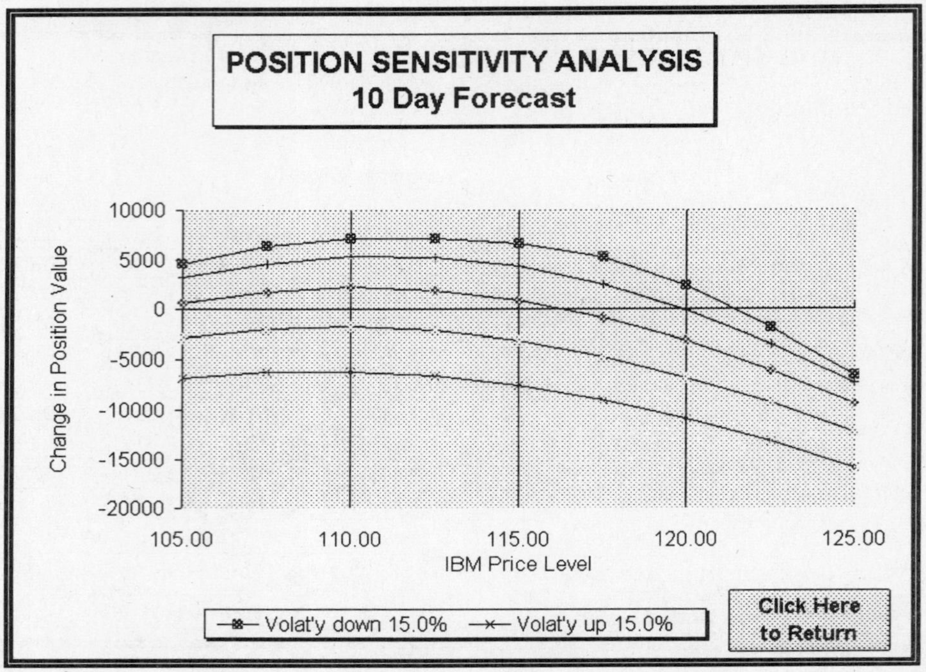
POSITION SENSITIVITY ANALYSIS
10 Day Forecast
10000
5000
0
-5000
-10000
-15000
-20000
Change in Position Value
105.00
110.00
115.00
120.00
125.00
IBM Price Level
Volat'y down 15.0%
Volat'y up 15.0%
Click Here to Return

From the graph, we can determine how far the underlying can move together with volatility so that we break even or better (i.e., our change in position value is positive or zero). We can also better understand how sensitive our position is to each of the underlying risk factors we chose.

Test your understanding of this worksheet by completing the *Problems to Accompany Options Risk Analysis*, which appears later in this manual.

Worksheet 12
Margin Account Simulator
Specific Instructions and a Numerical Example

MARGINS.XLS

This spreadsheet is designed to help the student understand futures margin accounts and how they work. The student should verify the calculations in the spreadsheet to gain the greatest possible educational benefit. Securities bought on margin exhibit much greater risk than securities paid in full with cash. This spreadsheet demonstrates exactly how much greater risk margin transactions can have when risk is measured in terms of variability in percentage gains and losses. All the calculations are done in a simulator environment; there are abundant opportunities for gains, losses, and margin calls!

The organization of the spreadsheet is similar to others in the package:

Menu:	This button returns you to the *Margins Menu* screen.

The *Menu* screen permits navigation to the following sections:

Intro:	Introduction to the worksheet
Market:	Provide market information
Simulator Data:	Provide simulator data
Simulator:	The step-by-step simulation routine
Accounts:	Sensitivity analysis settings
Dollars:	Graph showing security and margin values
Percentages:	Graph of percent changes
Reset:	Try a new simulation
Print:	Print your results
Quit:	Return to *The Innovative Investor* menu

The introductory screen appears below:

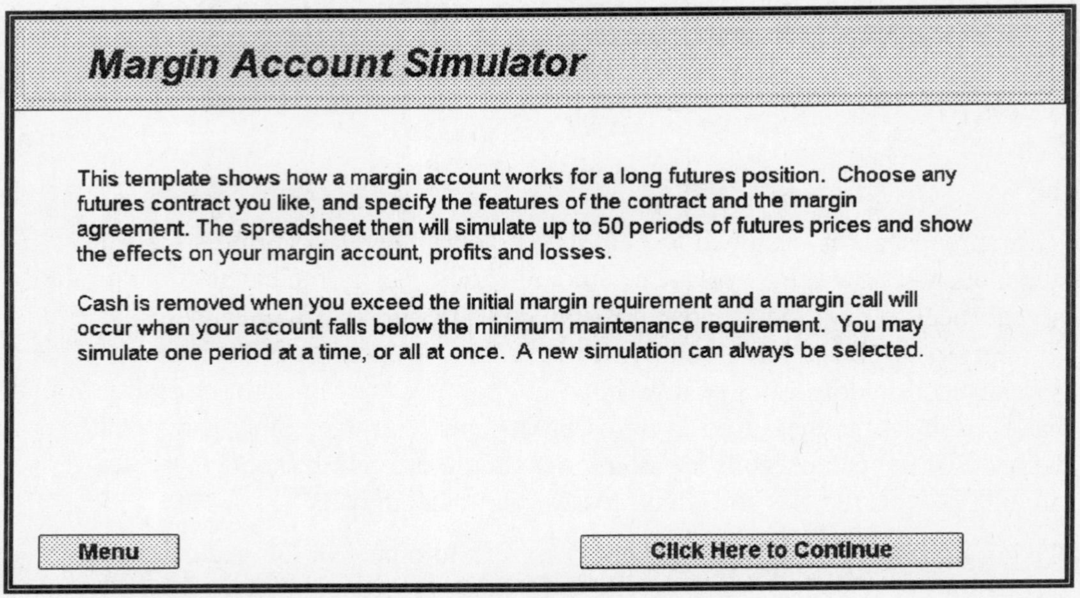
Margin Account Simulator
This template shows how a margin account works for a long futures position. Choose any futures contract you like, and specify the features of the contract and the margin agreement. The spreadsheet then will simulate up to 50 periods of futures prices and show the effects on your margin account, profits and losses.
Cash is removed when you exceed the initial margin requirement and a margin call will occur when your account falls below the minimum maintenance requirement. You may simulate one period at a time, or all at once. A new simulation can always be selected.
Menu
Click Here to Continue

There are two data screens. One provides information about the futures contract and margin account, and the other provides information about the simulation. We chose to study the S&P 500 futures contract, with prices from the end of February 1992. The S&P futures level at that time was 415, and the futures contract is settled based on 500 times the index. Here is the futures data screen and its corresponding *Help* screen.

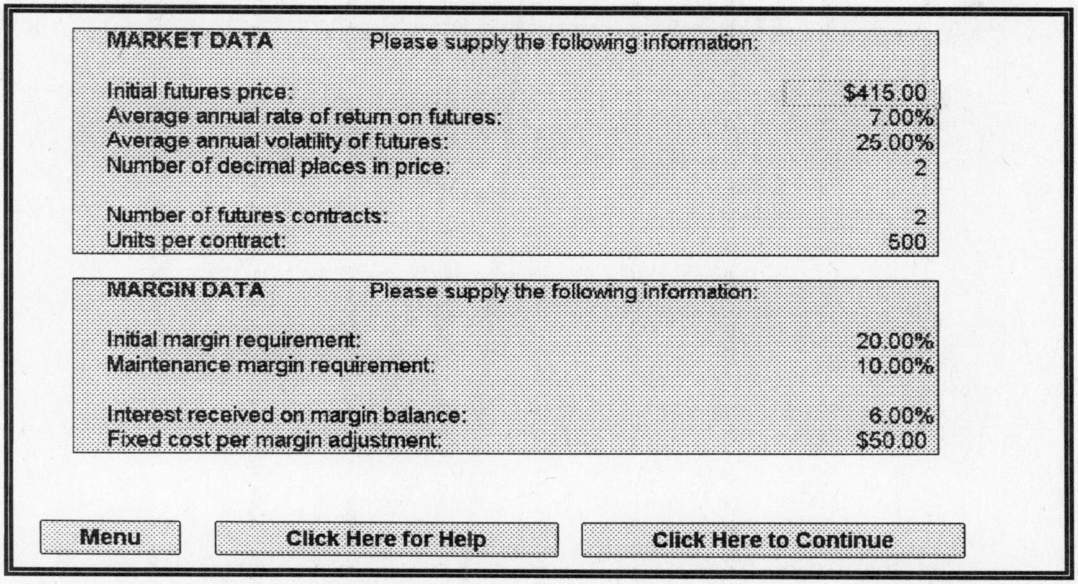
MARKET DATA
Please supply the following information:
Initial futures price:
$415.00
Average annual rate of return on futures:
7.00%
Average annual volatility of futures:
25.00%
Number of decimal places in price:
2
Number of futures contracts:
2
Units per contract:
500
MARGIN DATA
Please supply the following information:
Initial margin requirement:
20.00%
Maintenance margin requirement:
10.00%
Interest received on margin balance:
6.00%
Fixed cost per margin adjustment:
$50.00
Menu
Click Here for Help
Click Here to Continue

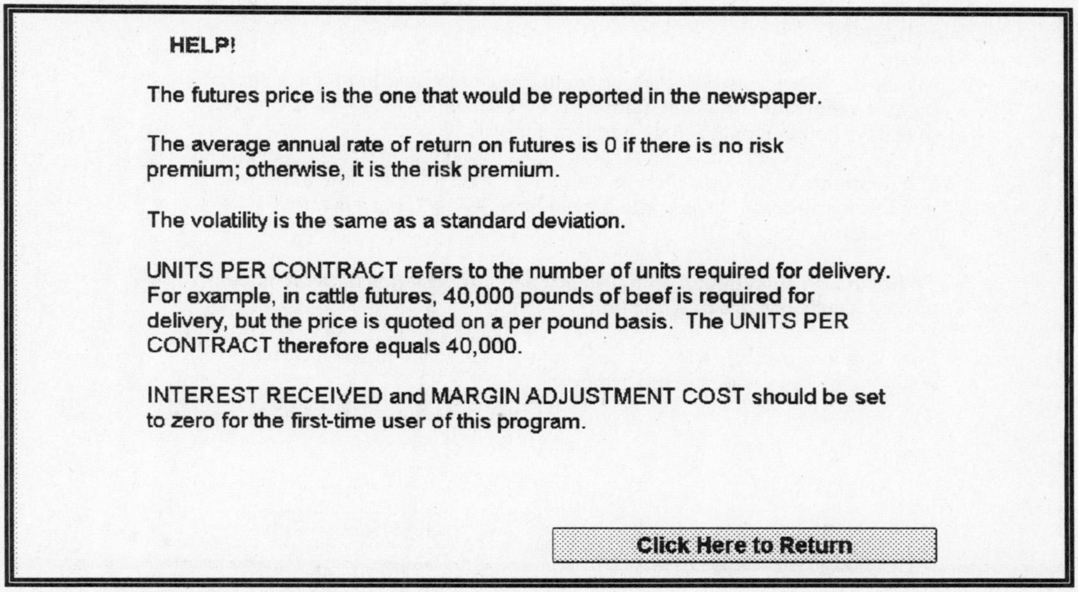
HELP!
The futures price is the one that would be reported in the newspaper.
The average annual rate of return on futures is 0 if there is no risk premium; otherwise, it is the risk premium.
The volatility is the same as a standard deviation.
UNITS PER CONTRACT refers to the number of units required for delivery. For example, in cattle futures, 40,000 pounds of beef is required for delivery, but the price is quoted on a per pound basis. The UNITS PER CONTRACT therefore equals 40,000.
INTEREST RECEIVED and MARGIN ADJUSTMENT COST should be set to zero for the first-time user of this program.
Click Here to Return

The second data screen requires that you provide the information about the simulation itself. Do you want to simulate one step at a time or all at once? In case you need more help interpreting the numbers, click the **Click Here for Help** button.

SIMULATOR DATA Please supply the following information:

Frequency of margin account revision (times/yr):	52
Number of periods to simulate: (Max 50)	50
Which simulation style should be used?	1
1 - One period at a time	
2 - All periods at once	

REFERENCE VALUES (Do not change)

Initial base value:	$415,000
Initial margin:	$83,000
Current maintenance margin:	$41,500

Menu | Click Here for Help | Click Here for Simulator

HELP!

In real life, margin accounts are updated daily. In order to see the effect of big price movements on the margin account value, we allow you to choose to update your account at less frequent intervals.

We recommend that you choose SIMULATION STYLE #1 the first time you use the program. It is a little slower than Style #2, but it is more informative.

To get the greatest benefit from this program, be sure you understand how all the calculations are determined.

For more information on margins and margin accounts, please consult your Bodie, Kane and Marcus textbook.

Click Here to Return

We strongly recommend you simulate one step at a time, at least for the first time you run the program. Later you can take as many steps as you want by typing the desired number of steps into the first column in the starting period row (the highlighted number).

The beginning simulation screen shows you the current status of your account:

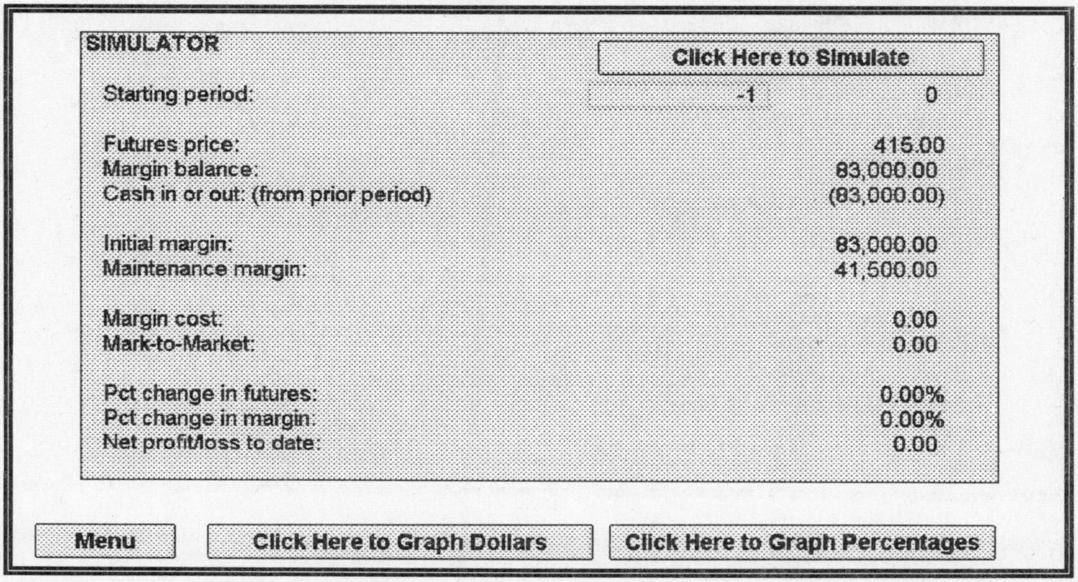
SIMULATOR
Click Here to Simulate
Starting period:
-1
0
Futures price:
415.00
Margin balance:
83,000.00
Cash in or out: (from prior period)
(83,000.00)
Initial margin:
83,000.00
Maintenance margin:
41,500.00
Margin cost:
0.00
Mark-to-Market:
0.00
Pct change in futures:
0.00%
Pct change in margin:
0.00%
Net profit/loss to date:
0.00
Menu
Click Here to Graph Dollars
Click Here to Graph Percentages

Click the **Click Here to Simulate** button to take a one-period step with your simulator. In the process of doing this, try to understand the basis for your gains and losses and how the margin account is settled. At any time, you may use **Graph Dollars** or **Graph Percentages** buttons to see what your dollar and percentage profits and losses turned out to be. Let's go forward 27 or so periods (your results will differ; your big loss may come sooner or later than 27 steps).

We had a pretty big loss in the 27th period. Wait, is that the telephone ringing? It's the broker with a margin call.

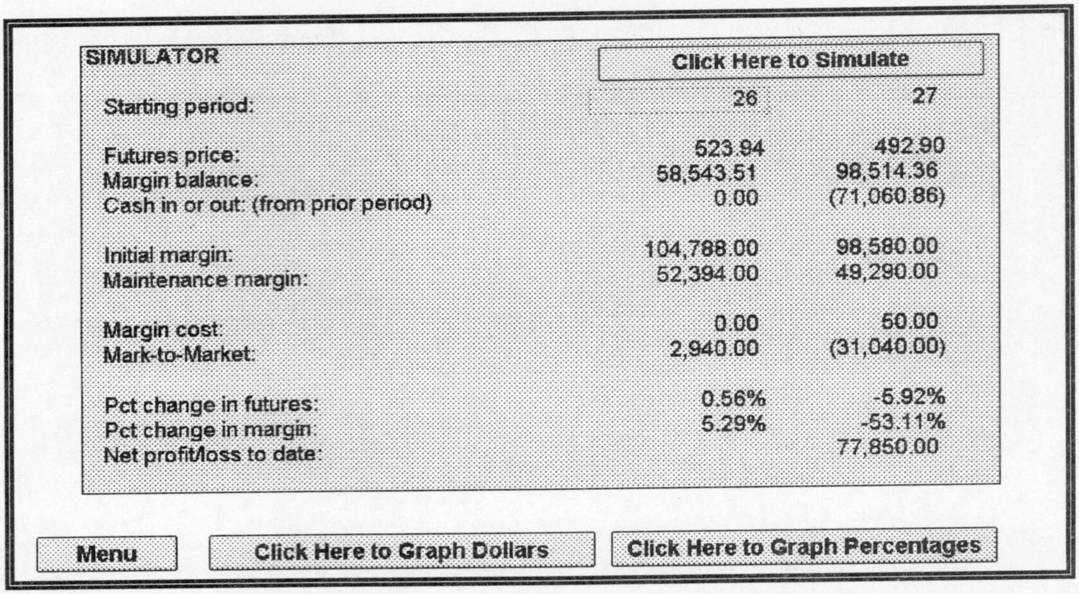
SIMULATOR
Click Here to Simulate
Starting period: 26 27
Futures price: 523.94 492.90
Margin balance: 58,543.51 98,514.36
Cash in or out: (from prior period) 0.00 (71,060.86)
Initial margin: 104,788.00 98,580.00
Maintenance margin: 52,394.00 49,290.00
Margin cost: 0.00 50.00
Mark-to-Market: 2,940.00 (31,040.00)
Pct change in futures: 0.56% -5.92%
Pct change in margin: 5.29% -53.11%
Net profit/loss to date: 77,850.00
Menu
Click Here to Graph Dollars
Click Here to Graph Percentages

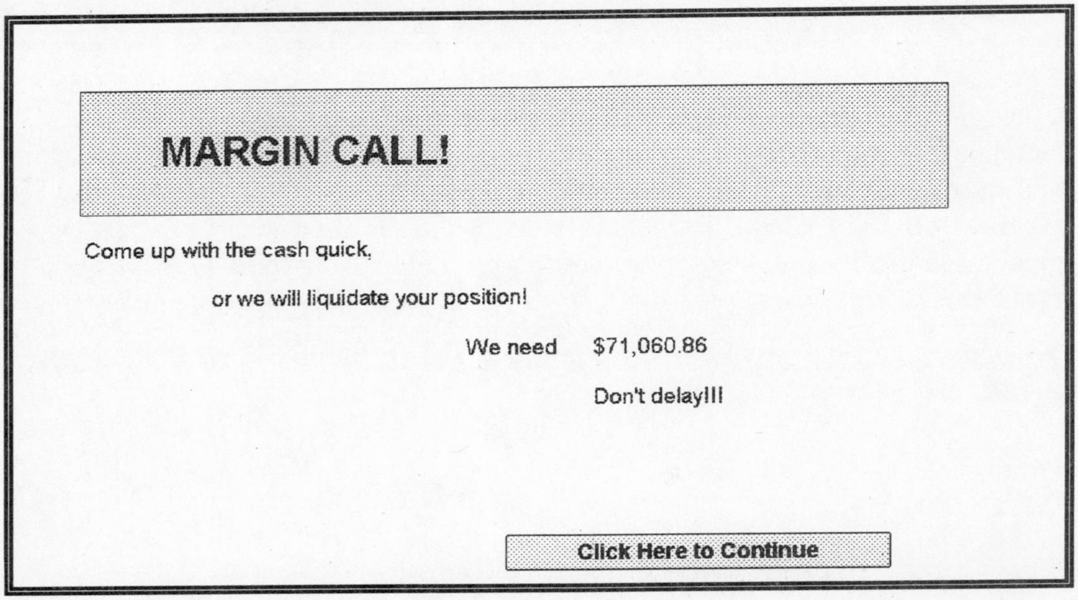
MARGIN CALL!
Come up with the cash quick,
or we will liquidate your position!
We need $71,060.86
Don't delay!!!
Click Here to Continue

Return to the *Menu* screen and click the **Accounts** button to review your whole account to date. The small scroll bar at the top right of the window permits you to scroll through all of the periods. After 27 periods, here's what we saw:

PERIODIC ACCOUNT SUMMARY

Menu

Period	Futures Price	% Chg	Margin Balance	% Chg	Cash In/Out
0	415.00	0	$83,000	0	($83,000)
1	443.52	6.87%	88,611	34.36%	22,909
2	454.35	2.44%	90,771	12.22%	8,670
3	443.35	-2.42%	79,771	-12.12%	0
4	441.36	-0.45%	77,781	-2.49%	0
5	435.44	-1.34%	71,861	-7.61%	0
6	456.11	4.75%	91,141	28.76%	1,389
7	461.63	1.21%	92,224	6.06%	4,438
8	500.54	8.43%	100,005	42.19%	31,129
9	482.24	-3.66%	81,705	-18.30%	0
10	474.58	-1.59%	74,045	-9.38%	0
11	487.82	2.79%	87,285	17.88%	0
12	476.08	-2.41%	75,545	-13.45%	0
13	469.08	-1.47%	68,545	-9.27%	0
14	463.89	-1.11%	63,355	-7.57%	0
15	489.41	5.50%	88,875	40.28%	0
16	478.10	-2.31%	77,565	-12.73%	0
17	469.38	-1.82%	68,845	-11.24%	0
18	505.90	7.78%	101,103	53.05%	4,262
19	531.24	5.01%	106,135	25.06%	20,308
20	543.41	2.29%	108,563	11.47%	9,742
21	538.75	-0.86%	103,903	-4.29%	0
22	581.60	7.95%	116,204	41.24%	30,549
23	547.59	-5.85%	82,194	-29.27%	0
24	558.93	2.07%	93,534	13.80%	0
25	521.00	-6.79%	55,604	-40.55%	0
26	523.94	0.56%	58,544	5.29%	0
27	492.90	-5.92%	98,514	-53.11%	(71,061)
28	0.00	0.00%	0	0.00%	0
29	0.00	0.00%	0	0.00%	0

Up to period 27, here are the graphical relationships we found:

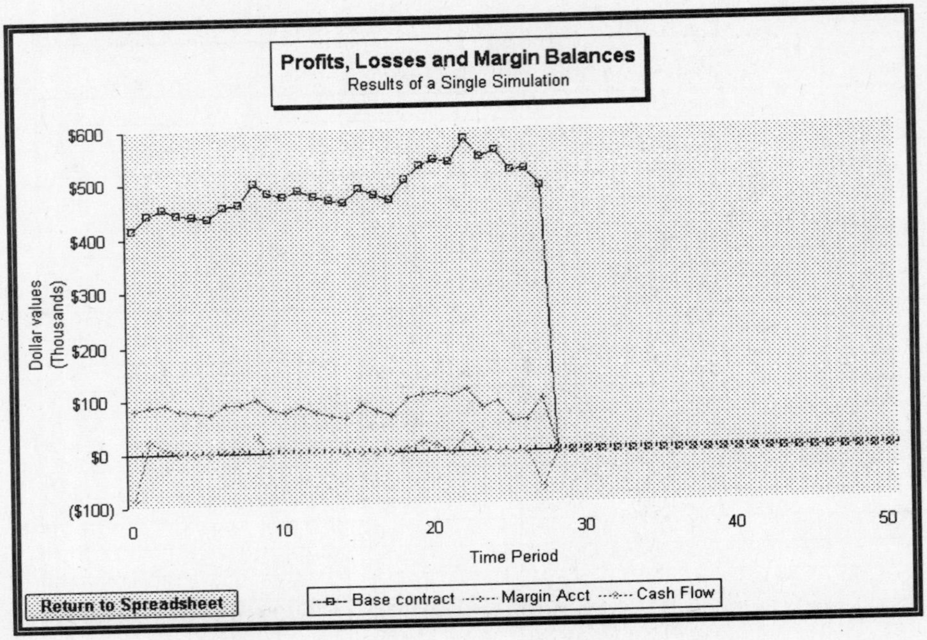
Profits, Losses and Margin Balances
Results of a Single Simulation
$600
$500
$400
$300
$200
$100
$0
($100)
Dollar values (Thousands)
0
10
20
30
40
50
Time Period
Return to Spreadsheet
Base contract
Margin Acct
Cash Flow

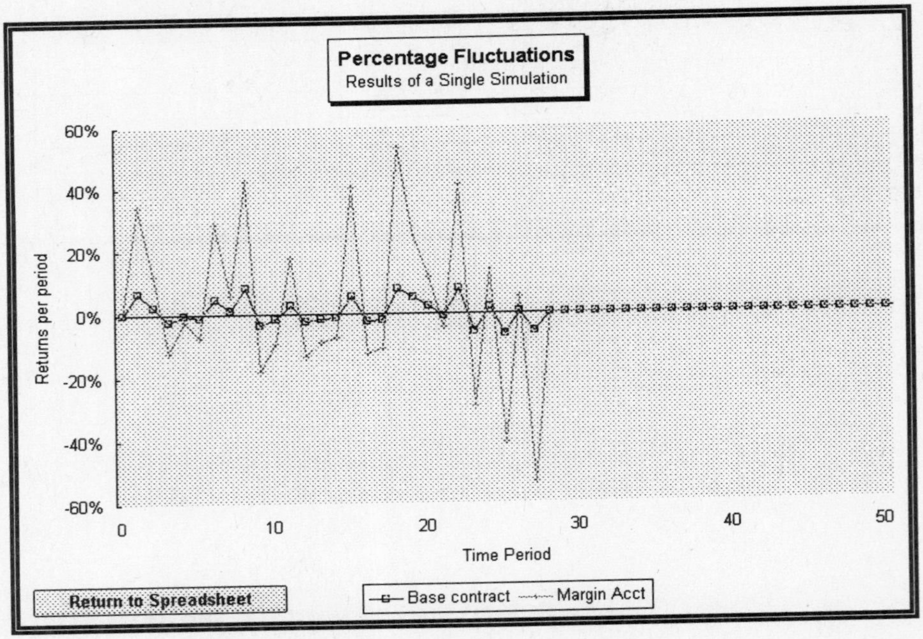
Percentage Fluctuations
Results of a Single Simulation
60%
40%
20%
0%
-20%
-40%
-60%
Returns per period
0
10
20
30
40
50
Time Period
Return to Spreadsheet
Base contract
Margin Acct

What can you conclude about the variability of margin accounts compared to the variability of futures prices? Test your understanding of this worksheet by completing the *Problems to Accompany Margin Account Simulator*, which appears later in this manual.

Worksheet 13
Quick European Option Pricing
Specific Instructions and a Numerical Example

QUICKOPT.XLS

This worksheet allows the user to easily calculate European option values using the Black-Scholes formula. Continuous proportional dividends are also allowed. Implied volatility calculations are automatic. For a given striking price and maturity, the user can establish a position involving calls, puts and shares of stock. Sensitivity analysis allows the student to determine the effect of changes in his assumptions on the value of his portfolio.

The menu options available are as follows:

Intro:	Introduction and background information for the worksheet
Calcs:	The basic Black-Scholes value and implied volatility calculator
Position:	Assemble a position of calls, puts, and stocks
What-if?:	Conduct sensitivity analysis for your position
Graph:	Graph your sensitivity analysis
Print:	Print selected results
Quit:	Return to *The Innovative Investor Master Menu*

The three introductory screens discuss some of the details of the Black-Scholes model, its underlying assumptions, and its adaptation to the payment of dividends. The user should consult the references at the end of the introduction for further information. The first screen is reached by clicking the **Intro** button.

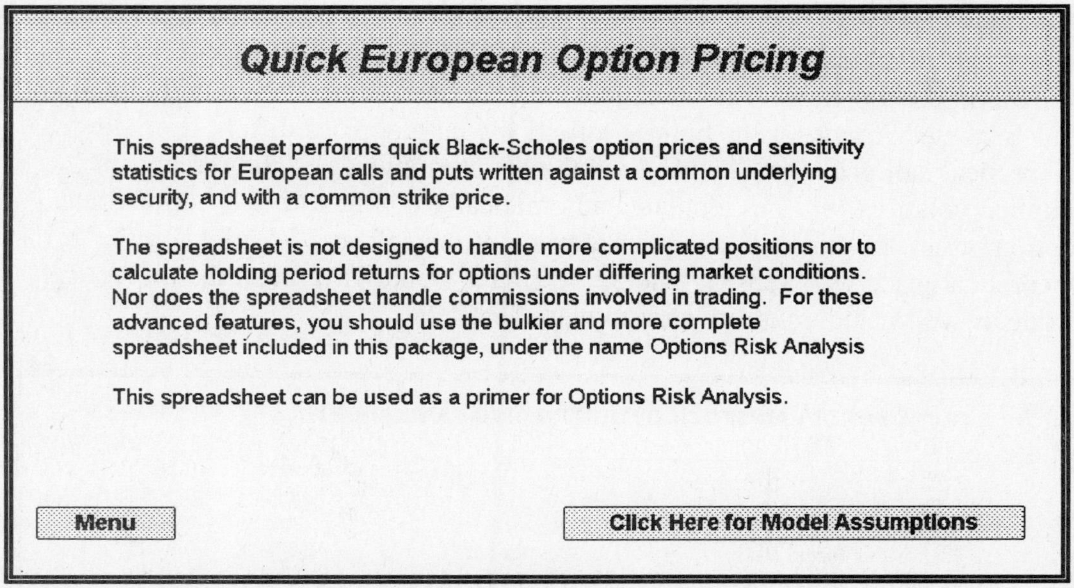
Quick European Option Pricing
This spreadsheet performs quick Black-Scholes option prices and sensitivity statistics for European calls and puts written against a common underlying security, and with a common strike price.
The spreadsheet is not designed to handle more complicated positions nor to calculate holding period returns for options under differing market conditions. Nor does the spreadsheet handle commissions involved in trading. For these advanced features, you should use the bulkier and more complete spreadsheet included in this package, under the name Options Risk Analysis
This spreadsheet can be used as a primer for Options Risk Analysis.
Menu
Click Here for Model Assumptions

If you click on the **Calcs** button in the *Menu* screen or the **Click Here to Continue** button in the third *Intro* screen, you will obtain the basic computation screen.

You may change any of the six inputs that appear in the shaded block in the upper half of the screen. The intermediate calculations (d_1, $N(d_1)$, etc.), are shown on the top right. The valuations and derivatives are shown in the shaded block labeled *Results* at the bottom left. If the market price differs from the theoretical call price, put its value on the lower-right side of the screen; the implied volatility will be calculated automatically (along with the implied put option price). In this case, the market price of the call was \$2.50 when the theoretical price was \$2.075. The \$2.50 figure would have been the theoretical value as well if the volatility chosen were 39.64%.

QUICK EUROPEAN STOCK OPTION PRICING WORKSHEET

Current Stock Price	$41.13	
Exercise Price	$45.00	
Time to Maturity	0.3300	yrs
Risk-free Interest Rate	5.00%	per yr
Volatility of Stock Price	35.00%	per yr
Continuous Dividend Yield	0.00%	per yr

d1	-0.2653
N(d1)	0.3954
d2	-0.4663
N(d2)	0.3205
S*	$41.13

RESULTS:	Theoreticals	
	Call	Put
Black-Scholes prices	$2.075	$5.213
Delta (per $1 underlying)	0.395	-0.605
Gamma (Delta / $1 underlying	0.047	0.047
Kappa (per 1% volatility)	0.091	0.091
Zeta (per 1% interest rate)	0.047	-0.099
Theta (per year time passage	5.535	3.321

Market overrides	
Call	Put
2.500	5.639

Implied volatility
39.64%

Click Here to Match

Menu

Click Here to Continue

If you calculate implied volatility and want to substitute implied volatility for the volatility you originally provided, simply click the **Click Here to Match** button to do so automatically.

We now wish to study some comparative statics. The *Position* screen permits us to indicate which variable we want to study (other than the underlying stock, which is included automatically). We may also specify a position. In the following case, I wanted to study call option values, so my position consisted of a single call option.

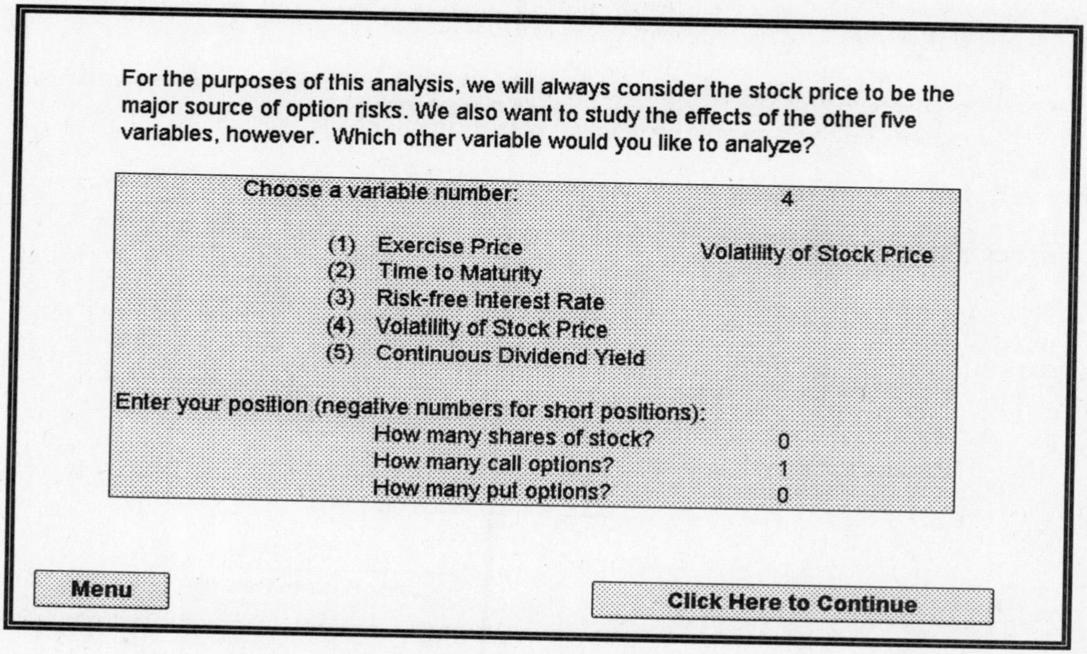
For the purposes of this analysis, we will always consider the stock price to be the major source of option risks. We also want to study the effects of the other five variables, however. Which other variable would you like to analyze?
Choose a variable number:
4
(1) Exercise Price
(2) Time to Maturity
(3) Risk-free Interest Rate
(4) Volatility of Stock Price
(5) Continuous Dividend Yield
Volatility of Stock Price
Enter your position (negative numbers for short positions):
How many shares of stock?
0
How many call options?
1
How many put options?
0
Menu
Click Here to Continue

The *What-if?* analysis portion gives the calculations below. You should choose a minimum stock price and a step size — altogether, five stock prices will be shown, and five values for the variable you specified earlier. If you want to change the settings and recalculate the table, simply enter the new values and click the **Click Here to Recalculate Table** button.

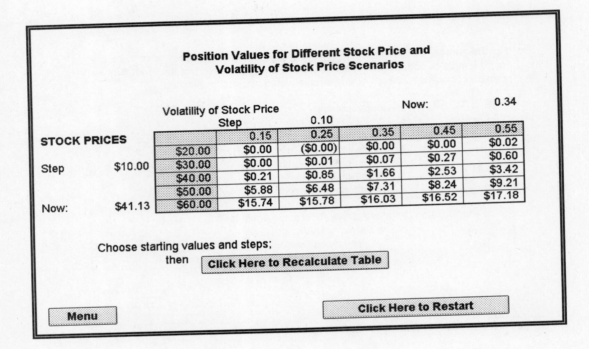

Position Values for Different Stock Price and Volatility of Stock Price Scenarios

Volatility of Stock Price

Step 0.10

Now: 0.34

STOCK PRICES

Step $10.00

Now: $41.13

	0.15	0.25	0.35	0.45	0.55
$20.00	$0.00	($0.00)	$0.00	$0.00	$0.02
$30.00	$0.00	$0.01	$0.07	$0.27	$0.60
$40.00	$0.21	$0.85	$1.66	$2.53	$3.42
$50.00	$5.88	$6.48	$7.31	$8.24	$9.21
$60.00	$15.74	$15.78	$16.03	$16.52	$17.18

Choose starting values and steps;
then **Click Here to Recalculate Table**

Menu

Click Here to Restart

The graphical portion of the *What-if?* analysis can be accessed from the *Menu* screen with the **Graph** button. The graph is shown below.

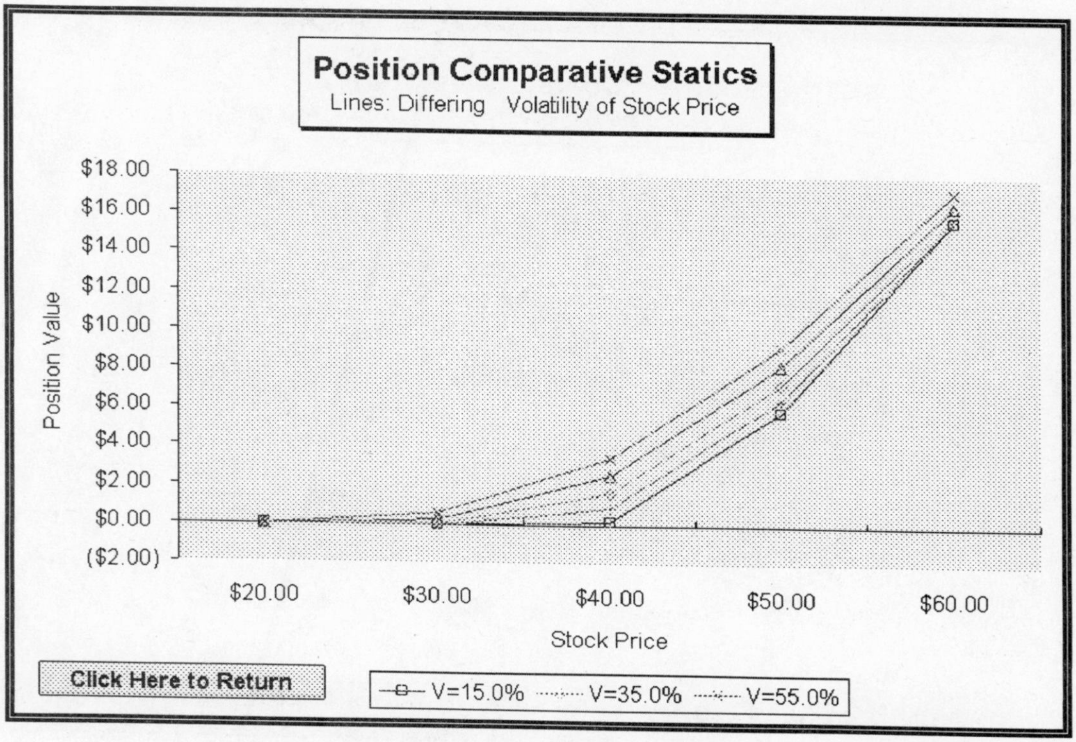
Position Comparative Statics
Lines: Differing Volatility of Stock Price
$18.00
$16.00
$14.00
$12.00
$10.00
$8.00
$6.00
$4.00
$2.00
$0.00
($2.00)
Position Value
$20.00
$30.00
$40.00
$50.00
$60.00
Stock Price
Click Here to Return
V=15.0%
V=35.0%
V=55.0%

Just for variety, we might also have examined a position that was short two calls and short two puts. If we had chosen that position, the *What-if?* graph would have looked like this:

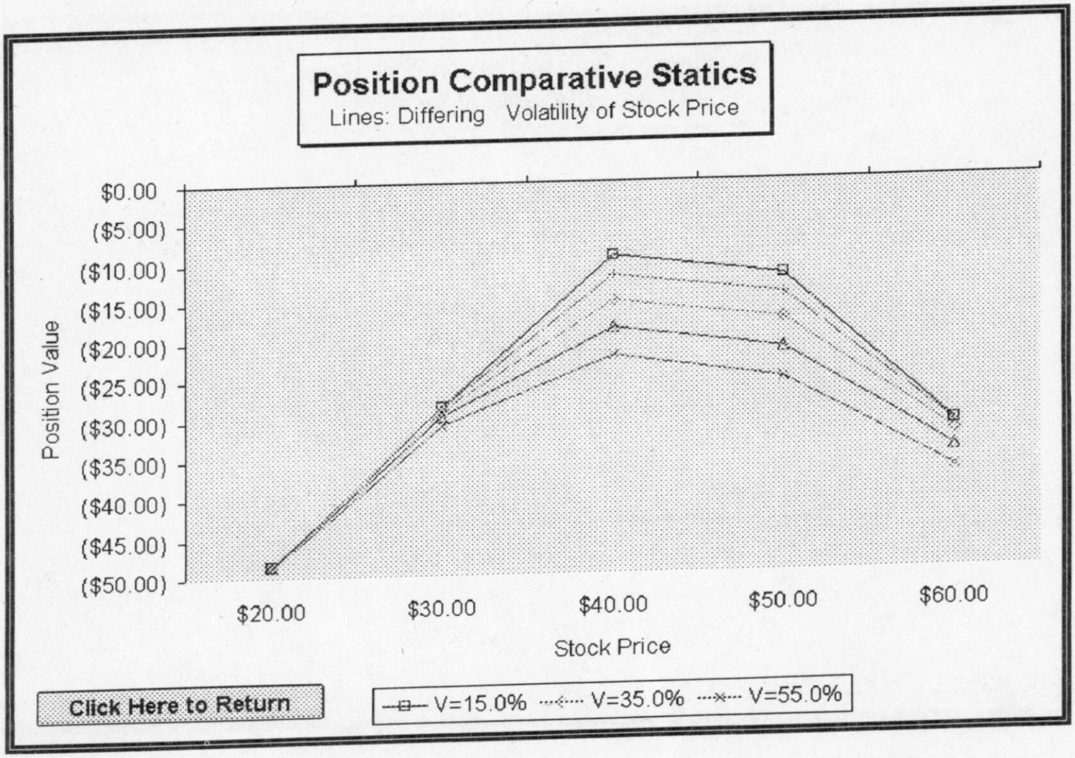
Position Comparative Statics
Lines: Differing Volatility of Stock Price
$0.00
($5.00)
($10.00)
($15.00)
($20.00)
($25.00)
($30.00)
($35.00)
($40.00)
($45.00)
($50.00)
Position Value
$20.00
$30.00
$40.00
$50.00
$60.00
Stock Price
Click Here to Return
V=15.0%
V=35.0%
V=55.0%

This is a simple and easy-to-use general Black-Scholes option pricing package. Test your understanding of this worksheet by completing the ***Problems to Accompany Quick European Option Pricing***, which appears later in this manual.

Problem Sets to Accompany The Innovative Investor

Problems to Accompany the Efficient Portfolio Frontier

Asset Allocation Problems

The following problems should be solved using *The Innovative Investor* worksheet *Efficient Portfolio Frontier*. (effport.xls)

Expected risk and return figures for the following assets: (Stocks, Bonds, Real Estate and Gold)

	Stocks	Bonds	R.E.	Gold
Expected Return (HPR)	14.8%	8.0%	10.6%	6.5%
Standard Deviation	.28	.17	.19	.12

Correlation Coefficients

	Stocks	Bonds	R.E.	Gold
Stocks	1.0	-.22	-.08	.08
Bonds		1.0	.19	-.04
R.E.			1.0	-.05
Gold				1.0

Assume you are managing a portfolio and may choose any combination of the assets listed above (including short selling). For each of the following questions, derive and print the composition of each portfolio and print the Efficient Frontier Graph.

1. Your client is very risk averse and desires to hold the lowest risk portfolio possible. Derive the portfolio and print the results (risk may be measured in terms of variance).

2. Suppose that you realize that the correlation coefficient between Real Estate and Bonds is 0.90, not the previously reported figure of 0.19. Given this change, derive the new minimum variance portfolio. (hint: short selling is involved) How reasonable is it to short sell the asset listed and how would you go about doing so?

For the following questions assume that you have the ability to both short sell and invest (i.e. borrow and lend) treasury securities at the risk free rate of 5.0%. Reverse the worksheet changes made in question #2 and click **Perform Calculations** in step 3 of the worksheet before answering the following questions.

3. Given the introduction of the risk free treasury asset, derive the tangency portfolio. Perform a simple sensitivity analysis by raising and lowering the risk free rate from the 5.0% benchmark. How does the Reward/Variability figure change and what does this tell you about the relationship between the slope of the tangency line and risk/return tradeoffs?

4. Your client is a Risk Neutral investor (i.e. they make investment decisions based on their desired expected rate of return, regardless of risk) and informs you that they want to earn 25%. Using only those portfolios that lie on the efficient frontier and your ability short sell a security, derive the target portfolio that best meets your client's needs.

5. Suppose that your client has a risk aversion level parameterized by A=4.0. Given the existence of a risk free asset, derive the optimal portfolio. Derive the optimal portfolio given risk aversion levels of A=2.0 and A=6.0. For each risk aversion level, note where you are on the tangency line, relative to the tangency portfolio, and explain the interaction with the risk free asset (hint: note the line called "wts" in step 7 of the worksheet).

6. (Harder) Now suppose that you can lend at 5%, but must borrow at 7%. Derive the tangency portfolio at each interest rate. Hand sketch the tangency line developed by combining these both the 5% and 7% tangency lines (hint: for points between the two tangency portfolios, it is necessary to "run along" the efficient frontier between the two tangency points). Find the asset weights, expected returns, and standard deviations of the optimal portfolios for investors with risk aversion parameters of 0.5, 4, and 10. Which risk free rate did you use for the A=4 case and why?

Problems to Accompany the Super Efficient Portfolio Frontier

Constrained Portfolio Optimization

The following problems should be solved using *The Innovative Investor* worksheet *The Super Efficient Portfolio.* (supereff.xls)

For the following questions, refer to the data set provided in the section titled *The Efficient Portfolio Frontier* (effport.xls) The risk free rate used is 5.0%.

1. Derive the optimal portfolio composition, given risk aversion parameters of 4 and 12. If the investor does not have the ability to borrow or lend at the risk free rate, how does the composition of the portfolio change?

2. Answer #1 again, assuming the expected return on Gold is 3.0%. (Remember to *recalculate.*) What aspect is now added to your portfolio that was not previously included?

3. Change the return on Gold back to 6.5% (and *recalculate*). As the manager of a pension fund, you have the following limitations: Gold holdings may not exceed 5% and Real Estate holdings may not exceed 20%. Without borrowing or lending, derive the composition of your optimal portfolio. How does your answer change if you can borrow or lend funds?

4. You manage a bond fund, which must hold at least 85% bonds. Derive the composition of your optimal portfolio with and without borrowing/lending.

5. Develop your own set of constraints. Explain why you selected these limitations and derive the composition of the optimal portfolio.

Problems To Accompany Index Models and Performance

Beta Book and Portfolio Performance Evaluation

The following problems should be solved using *The Innovative Investor* worksheet *Index Models and Performance.* (index.xls)

On the Beta Book Data screen, click on **PREPARE CRUNCH DATA**. Use *pdata.xls* as the data file and *DJDATA* as the worksheet in crunch wizard step 2. Select the top left data point as your cell reference. Select VWCRSP as the benchmark and any other five stocks as the securities to evaluate. Data occur in monthly frequencies and in the form of net returns. (Value Weighted Index calculated by the Center for Research in Security Prices at the University of Chicago will be used as a proxy for the market portfolio.)

Click on **LOAD CRUNCH DATA** and proceed to question 1.

1. Print the Beta Book Data. How is the alpha from the beta book derived? How does this relate to our notion of the distance between the expected return and the security market line (i.e. the financial alpha)? If you assume the average financial alpha is zero, what does that imply about the risk-free rate and the required return on the market, assuming the CAPM is true? What does the SML graph look like in this case?

2. If you change the average financial alpha to be something other than zero, what does that imply about the securities you chose? What might it imply about the single-factor CAPM?

3. Calculate the total return variance for each of the securities you chose. According to the CAPM, what percentage of the risk of each of these securities is diversifiable?

4. For which securities is the beta significantly different from zero (in a statistical sense)? What about the financial alpha?

5. (Harder) You are the pension fund director at a corporation with a $100M pension fund. You solicited four equity managers for their investment performance results (after cost) in the last 6 years. You wish to compare their results to the benchmark of the S&P 500 return:

S&P	A	B	C	D
12%	16%	11%	-3%	7%
-6%	-20%	-8%	18%	9%
25%	26%	22%	5%	8%
2%	4%	3%	-1%	6%
-19%	-17%	-20%	25%	8%
5%	-3%	2%	4%	7%

a. How would you describe each manager's investment strategy?
b. Calculate and rank the four performance measures for each of the managers. Print out your results in tabular and graphical form.
c. Make an informed recommendation as to the manager your corporation should hire.

HINT: Consult the section on how to use your own data file in *Crunch*.

Problems to Accompany Bond Risk Analysis

Bond Portfolio Management

The following problems should be solved using *The Innovative Investor* worksheet *Bond Risk Analysis.* (bondrisk.xls)

Problem:

Your bond portfolio consists of the following treasury securities. Listed is the relevant price data as of June 20, 1997.

Qty	Coupon	Maturity	Bid	Ask	YTM
13	5-1/8	Jun 1998	99-13	99-16	5.62
8	6-3/4	Jun 1999	101-13	101-16	5.94
20	6-5/8	Jun 2001	101-12	101-15	6.20
26	7	Jul 2006	103-28	103-31	6.41

When entering the date, use the full four-digit year. List prices as their decimal equivalent. Make sure that price, quote and pmt at maturity are the same denomination - i.e. $100s or $1000s.)

1. On June 20, 1997, what is the accrued interest, the bond invoice, and computed yields for each bond? Why are the computed yields different than the YTM listed in the quote from the newspaper?

2. Given the duration and convexity listed in the worksheet, compute the value of your portfolio now and given a 1% rise in interest rates.

3. The Federal Reserve Board has announced a concern about inflation. You are considering a hedge against a rise in interest rates. You have two portfolios with which to hedge. Portfolio 1 consists of the same bonds in quantities of (3,1,18,30) and Portfolio 2 consists of the same bonds in quantities of (15,19,3,8). How does the value of each portfolio change given a 0.50% rise in interest rates?

4. (Harder) Recall that hedging is the act of creating an equal and opposite price movement, in order to reduce/eliminate volatility. What strategy and which hedge portfolio would you use to hedge the 0.50% rise listed in #3.

5. (Harder) Suppose that Portfolio 2 was your only option to create a hedge. But, you have the ability to alter the quantity of holdings in bonds 3 & 4. What would be the quantity of each bond in the newly created hedge portfolio? (Remember to use the *?* feature.)

Problems to Accompany Term Structure

Term Structure of Interest Rates

The following problems should be solved using *The Innovative Investor* worksheet *Term Structure Analysis*. (termstr.xls)

Assume "Today's date = June 20, 1997" for all questions.

Below is Treasury Bond and Treasury Note closing price information as of June 20, 1997 (all prices are listed in 32nds):

Coupon	Maturity	Bid	Ask	Change	YTM
5-1/8	Jun 1998	99-13	99-16	0	5.62
6-3/4	Jun 1999	101-13	101-16	+ 01	5.94
5-7/8	Jun 2000	99-10	99-13	+ 02	6.09
7-1/2	May 2002	105-07	105-10	+ 03	6.22
6-1/2	May 2002	100-31	101-01	+ 02	6.25
10-3/4	May 2003	121-17	121-20	+ 03	6.29
7-1/4	Aug 2004	105-01	105-04	+ 05	6.34
7	Jul 2006	103-28	103-31	+ 07	6.41
6-5/8	May 2007	101-27	101-29	+ 06	6.36
11-1/4	Feb 2015	147-06	147-10	- 13	6.65
6-1/4	Aug 2023	94-01	94-05	+ 10	6.73
6-5/8	Feb 2027	99-20	99-22	+ 12	6.65

1. Unless noted otherwise, all bonds are assumed to expire on the last day of the month in which they mature. Input the ask prices and bond data into the worksheet and determine the YTM, Duration, and Volatility for each bond.
   a. What is the relationship between duration and maturity?
   b. What is the relationship between duration and YTM?
   c. What is the relationship between duration and volatility?
   d. Explain why these relationships exist.
2. Calculate a term structure of interest rates using first time to maturity and then duration as the independent variable.
   a. Do you detect any qualitative differences between the graphs?
   b. Do you detect any unusual patterns in either graph?
   c. For the two bonds maturing in May 2002, which has the lower duration and why?
3. A new treasury security is being issued today (June 20, 1997). The annual coupon rate is 7%, paid every 6 months, starting November 30, 1997. The maturity is 20 years (or May 2017). Using the term structure derived in #1, calculate the price of the bond, the duration, and the YTM.

Problems to Accompany Quick Bond Valuation

Bond Pricing

The following problems should be solved using *The Innovative Investor* worksheet *Quick Bond Valuation.* (quikbond.xls)

Answer the following questions given these facts. A 15 year government bond ($1,000 par) pays a semiannual coupon of 4% (8% annually) and has a yield to maturity of 6.5%.

1. Compute the price, duration, modified duration, and convexity of this bond.
2. If the YTM increases to 7.0%, what is the new price of the bond? What is the relationship between your calculation and the modified duration?
3. If the YTM increases to 7.0%, what is the new duration of the bond? How is this figure related to the convexity calculation?
4. If the price of the bond increases by $30, what is the new YTM?
5. What is the nature of the relationship between yield and price?
6. How do each of the following affect the duration:
   a. an increase in the time to maturity
   b. an increase in the coupon rate
   c. an increase in the YTM
7. Perform a complete sensitivity analysis for your bond. Assuming that yields could change by as much as 3% (up or down) and projecting forward in time by as much as 5 years, predict the impact of changes in conditions on the value of the bond in #1. Repeat the exercise with the duration of the bond in place of the price. Show your results graphically.

Problems to Accompany Valuing Convertible Debt

Convertible Bond Pricing

The questions here can be found in the CONVPRIC.XLS worksheet itself, but are repeated here for convenience.

Questions on graphical interpretation:

1. Which of the three securities is always worth the most? Why?
2. Why is the straight bond always worth the least? In other words, why can't the value of the ________ option ever exceed the value of the ________ option?
3. At what firm value should the firm's management call the callable convertible debt?
4. If the firm has issued convertible debt and suddenly issues more (with exactly the same terms), what will happen to the diagram?
5. How does an increase in the volatility of the firm's assets affect the values of convertible securities? Print a graph under two different volatility scenarios.

Questions for discussion:

1. Start with an asset value of $200, volatility 50%, maturity date 10 years, $100 face valued debt, a 13% interest rate, a 15% dilution factor, and an 8% call price discount rate. If the firm has issued callable convertibles, and calls them now, what will the bondholders prefer to choose, cash or shares? Why?

1. Print out the balance sheet associated with A. Calculate the value of the bondholders' gains. Explain where the gains came from and why they took place.
2. Suppose the firm's value jumps to $400 because of a new discovery. Repeat steps A and B.

3. At what firm value should the company have called the debt? (This may take some experimentation.) What is the bondholder's gain in this case? Can you justify your answer intuitively?

Problems To Accompany Two-Dividend Growth Model

Two-Stage Dividend Growth

The following problems should be solved using *The Innovative Investor* worksheet *Two-Dividend Growth Model.* (twodiv.xls)

1. Dog Days, Inc. is expected to pay an annual dividend of $3.00 per share on June 30, 1997. The dividend is expected to grow at a rate of 6% per year for the next three years. The fifth year dividend, and every dividend thereafter, is expected to increase at 4% per year. If the risk free rate is 5%, the market return is 14%, Dog Days beta is 0.8, what is the estimated price of Dog Days, Inc. common stock on June 20, 1997? Calculate the price of Dog Days stock at various dates over the next two years.

2. Using the same data from #1, calculate the value of stock if the dividend is paid quarterly and the first dividend payment is expected to be $0.75 on June 30, 1997. Be careful when calculating the number of periods until the intermediate dividend.

3. Use the annual dividend numbers from #1. While you are confident in your forecast for Dog Days growth rates (both short term and long term), the experts' opinions vary within 1% in each direction on both numbers. What is a range of possible stock prices given various growth rates? Print the Sensitivity Analysis Graph and explain what is tells you about the range of possible stock prices.

4. (Harder) Most investors use figures, other than dividends, to calculate stock prices. *The Two-Dividend Growth Model* worksheet can still be used, if you use another figure (i.e. EPS or Cash Flow), as a proxy for dividends. Using actual current data and a dividend proxy, compute the price of a stock. Use different proxies until you calculate a price similar to the actual market price. What does this tell you about how the market derives the price for your stock?

Problems To Accompany Futures Pricing

Futures Valuation and Risk Management

The following problems should be solved using *The Innovative Investor* worksheet *Futures Pricing*. (futures.xls)

We wish to analyze the futures contract trading on the S&P 500 Index. Our analysis will incorporate the following data assumptions:

- Current value of S&P 500 Index = 898
- YTM on 30 day T-Bill = 5.00%
- Dividend Yield on S&P 500 = 3%
- Average annual growth in asset value of S&P 500 = 14.5%
- Volatility of average annual growth of S&P 500 = 28%

1. Given a futures price of 905, what is the cost of carry for the 3 month futures contract? Using this cost of carry, what are the theoretical prices for the 3 month, 6 month and 12 month futures contracts?

2. The reported price of the 3 month, 6 month, & 12 month contracts are 905, 914 and 935, respectively. Explain the difference between these prices and your theoretical prices.

3. What happens to the futures prices if (a) the index rises, (b) interest rates rise or (c) dividends rise? How can you explain these effects intuitively? When the index changes by 3%, what happens to the futures price?

4. Your portfolio's exposure to the S&P 500 Index is equivalent to holding 5 units of the S&P 500 underlying security. At the same time, you have decided to go short 4 contracts with one year to expiration. What happens to the value of your position if (a) the index rises, (b) interest rates rise or (c) dividends rise? How can you explain these effects intuitively? In one week, the index changes by 3%, what happens to the value of your position? What happens to the value of your position if not hedged?

5. Suppose you hold the position in #4 for one month. You are convinced the S&P 500 Index will rise 50 points, but are not sure what interest rates will do. For the sake of simplicity, assume that interest rates either do not change or they increase by 0.50% over the period. What are your projected gains and losses in the two scenarios? Why does the worksheet calculate two different forecasts and take the average?

6. Consider over the next month that the price of the S&P 500 Index may fall to between 800 and 840, and interest rates may end up between 4.75% and 5.50%. What are your forecast for profits and losses to the position established in #4? Plot your results. What generalizations can you make about the value of your position? What has to happen for your position to profit?

7. Simulate a path for the S&P 500 Index to take in the next 3 months, along with a 3 month futures contract. Where is the futures price in relation to the spot price? How can you describe the difference between the two as time passes? What would cause the futures price to fall below the S&P 500 Index value? Graph your simulation result.

Problems To Accompany Hedge Dynamics

Hedging Simulation

The following problems should be solved using *The Innovative Investor* worksheet *Hedging Dynamics*. (hedge.xls)

Objective: To see how well one can hedge a well-diversified stock portfolio against changes in interest and inflation rates using the lbbotson/Sinquefeld data supplied with this packet.

Click on **PREPARE CRUNCH DATA**. Use pdata.xls as the data file and IBBSIN as the worksheet in crunch wizard step 2. Select B1 as your cell reference. Select the stock returns as our hedged contract (or benchmark), and bond and inflation returns as our contracts used to perform a hedge (or Securities to Evaluate). Data occur in annual frequencies and in the form of net returns. We assume the existence of an asset that grows at exactly the rate of inflation reported in Ibbotson and Sinquefeld. Click on **LOAD CRUNCH DATA** and proceed to question 1.

2. Assuming returns are jointly normally distributed with constant parameters, what are the optimal hedge ratios? For a $100,000 investment in stocks, what are the recommended hedge ratios produced by the program using bonds and inflation?
3. Redo #1 using only bonds when preparing the Crunch data.
4. Simulate 25 future periods, allowing hedge re-adjustment for every period. Print a graph of the performance of the optimal hedge against your hedge. Which seemed to track the stock fund most closely?
   Print and interpret the summary statistics comparing the performance of the two hedges. Print out the actual profits and losses per period.

Problems to Accompany Options Risk Analysis

Advanced Option Pricing

All problems assume that the Black-Scholes model is the correct option pricing model, or, in the presence of stochastic volatility, the implied volatility generated by the Black-Scholes model shifts in a parallel fashion across the board. They should be solved using *The Innovative Investor* worksheet *Option Risk Analysis*. (optrisk.xls)

Below is the set of data for IBM options and common stock as of the close of trading on Friday, March 17, 1989. Also attached is a copy of the CBOE expiration calendar for 1989.

IBM Stock & Option		Calls (last)			Puts (last)		
Price	Strike	Mar	Apr	Jul	Mar	Apr	Jul
112 3/8	*105*	s	9 1/4	s	s	11/16	s
112 3/8	110	s	5 1/8	8 3/8	s	1 1/2	2 3/4
112 3/8	115	1/16	2 1/4	5 3/8	2 1/2	3 5/8	5 1/8
112 3/8	120	1/16	7/8	3 1/8	4	7 1/2	8 1/4
112 3/8	125	r	5/16	1 3/4	12 3/4	12 3/8	13
112 3/8	130	r	1/8	15/16	14	14	17 1/2
112 3/8	135	r	1/16	1/2	r	19	22

r - Not traded. s - No option.

For 1989 options stop trading on the following days: Jan 20, Feb 17, March 17, Apr 21, May 19, June 16, July 21, Aug 18, Sep 15, Oct 20, Nov 17, Dec 15. The options actually expire the following day.

1. Assuming you could trade at these prices, could you create any arbitrage opportunities? If you can, why hasn't the market done so already? Enter the April and July data into your worksheet with strike prices from 110 to 130. Assume the interest rate is 8% and there are no dividends.

   Calculate the implied volatility for IBM from these market prices. If these numbers differ by strike, why might they differ? If they differ from call to put on the same strike, why might they differ? Print out a table of prices and implied volatility.

2. Assume you hold the following position: Short 5 April 115 Puts, Short 7 Jul 120 Puts, Short 7 Jul 125 Calls, Short 5 Apr 130 Calls. Commissions per option (100 share) transaction are $25.

   Over a 10 day horizon, consider the following possible changes in market conditions and document the impact on your portfolio. (Assume you close out your position at the end of 10 days.) "Impact" implies change in value and risk parameters of the position. Try to justify each effect qualitatively as well as quantitatively. Why should each change in value have occurred? Consider each effect separately.

   a. Volatility increases 2% across the board
   b. IBM increases by $15 in value, but volatility drops by 1%.
   c. Interest rates drop by 2%.

3. For scenario (a) above, print a table of individual option deltas, Vegas, and Zetas. How does the change impact these risk factors. How can you back up your quantitative results with intuition?

4. Print a table and graph showing how your position value varies with changes in the underlying asset price and volatility. For what range of changes in the two variables will you break even or do better? For example, if implied volatility stays the same, for what range of underlying price will your position stay the same or gain value? Answer the same question for other possible volatility changes.

Problems to Accompany Margin Account Simulator

Futures Margining

The following problems should be solved using *The Innovative Investor* worksheet *Margin Account Simulator.* (margins.xls)

You are the treasurer at Quaker Oats. It has been decided that the corporation will hedge the price of its input grains by taking long positions in the corn and wheat futures market. You have been asked to provide some scenarios to determine what impact fluctuations in the market will have on the company's margin account.

The company will be long 50 corn futures contracts. Each contract calls for the delivery of 5,000 bushels of corn. The futures price of corn is currently $2.50 per bushel. The futures price grows at a rate of 0.2% per year on average, with an annualized volatility of 35%. Our initial margin requirement is 10% of the cash value of the contracts, and the maintenance margin is 5%. No interest is paid on your margin balance, and the cost per margin adjustment is $100 in addition to the adjustment. The account is settled weekly, and you've been asked to simulate for 50 weeks.

1. Do one sample simulation for 50 periods, one period at a time. What do you notice about the relationship between the futures price change and the margin account change?
2. If you had a margin call, describe the circumstances that lead to the margin call. What was your balance before and after the margin call in relation to the initial and maintenance margins?
3. For one period where the futures price increased, and for one where it decreased, show how the calculations in the account summary are made.
4. What is the net effect of the simulation you tried? What numbers would you use to best summarize this particular simulation?

Before completing the next problem, it might be wise to save a backup copy of the worksheet. Use the *Save As. . .* menu command. Do not save it under its given name, *margins.xls*, instead give it a new but related name such as *xmargin.xls*. This will prevent you from modifying the original worksheet in such a way that data or calculations are inadvertently lost.

4. (Harder) The worksheet can easily be modified to calculate the items you mentioned in #4. Modify the worksheet, then perform 10 simulations to see how variable your summary statistics are. (hint: For example, consider the most the company had to pay into a margin account in any given week. Is this relatively consistent across simulations, or are the results markedly different?)

Problems to Accompany Quick European Option Pricing

Beginning Option Pricing

All problems assume that the Black-Scholes model is the correct option pricing model. They should be solved using *The Innovative Investor* worksheet *Quick Option Pricing*. (quickopt.xls)

1. Assume the conditions leading to the Black-Scholes formula are true. What assumptions are made in calculating option prices under this formula?
2. What is the value of a McGraw Hill call option if McGraw Hill trades at 58, its volatility is 28% annually, the interest rate is 5%, the strike price is 62, and the option expires in 60 days? What is the price of a put? How much of each price represents intrinsic value and how much represents time value premium?
3. What is the value of one covered call position? (Note: Each position represents 100 shares and 100 calls. A covered call is one long stock position for each short call position.)
4. You are concerned how a rise in volatility would effect the value of your position. Construct a table given a starting volatility of 28%, increasing in increments of 5%. Print the table you produced and the graph that accompanies the table.
   a. How does the position value change when volatility rises? Why?
   b. After 10 days, the stock price rises to $62. If all other variables remain the same, what is the value of your position? If you expect the stock price to increase at least $2 and all other variables to remain constant until the option expires, when should you close your position? What will be the value of your position, and what is your profit? (Hint: Construct a sensitivity table using decreasing time to maturity as your variable.)

5. (Delta) Consider the original call option in #2. What is its delta? If the stock price were to increase $1.00, what is the change in value for the call? How do these two numbers compare? If they're different, why are they different?

6. (Kappa) Consider again the call option in #2. What is its vega? If the volatility of the stock price were to increase by 1.0%, what is the change in value for the call? How do these two numbers compare? If they're different, why are they different?

7. (Dividend Yield) Suppose that the conditions of #2 apply, but the continuous dividend yield for McGraw Hill is 2% annually. What is the impact of this increase in dividend yield on call and put prices? Can you justify the directions of these changes in prices intuitively?

8. The McGraw Hill call options listed in #2 are trading at a price of $1.75. What is the implied volatility? What is the market saying about its expectations concerning McGraw Hill's future price performance?

9. (Harder) You've just got some juicy, but unclear information on McGraw Hill. They are finalizing a merger with a major competitor and the announcement is scheduled for exactly 30 days from today. You know that the merger will be very good for one firm and bad for the other, you simply do not know which.
   a. Given the market conditions listed in #2, compute the value of a single Straddle Purchase position (i.e. one long call for every long put).
   b. What advantage do you obtain from a Straddle Purchase?
   c. Based on your position, all other variables constant, would you prefer a $10 rise or fall in the price of McGraw Hill and why?

Abbreviated Solutions

Problems to Accompany *The Innovative Investor*

This solution set is deliberately sketchy but full of hints. They are intended to show you that you are (presumably) on the right track.

The Efficient Portfolio Frontier

1. The minimum variance portfolio consists of the following asset weights:
   Stocks=11.1% Bonds=24.8% RE=17.1% Gold=47.0%

2. Weights S=13.4 B=43.8 R=(-10.4) G=53.2
   You can not short sell real property, therefore you must use a proxy such as a REIT.

3. The tangency portfolio consists of the following asset weights:
   Stocks=28.1 Bonds=24.3 RE=29.4 Gold=18.3
   Higher risk free rates mean lower R/V figures. Lower risk free rates mean higher R/V figures. This implies a steeper CAL. A steeper CAL implies higher returns at each level of risk. Thus, steeper is better.

4. The target portfolio consists of the following asset weights:
   Stocks=158.1 Bonds=19.9 RE=123.9 Gold=(-201.9)

5. A=4 S=36.8 B=31.8 R=38.5 G=24.0 TB=(-31)
   A=2 S=73.5 B=63.6 R=76.9 G=48.1 TB=(-162)
   A=6 S=24.5 B=21.2 R=25.6 G=16.0 TB=(+13)
   TB is t-bills at the risk free rate of 5%.
   The lower your risk aversion, the more you will borrow at the risk free rate.

6. Rf= 5.0% S=28.1 B=24.3 R=29.4 G=18.3
   Rf= 7.0% S=50.7 B=23.5 R=45.8 G=(-20.0)

   A=0.5 Rf=7.0% Er=33.6% StdDev=73.0%
   S=227.3 B=105.4 R=205.5 G=(-89.6) TB=(-349)

   A=10 Rf=5.0% Er=7.8% StdDev=5.3%
   S=14.7 B=12.7 R=15.4 G=9.6 TB=48

   A=4 Rf=none Er=11.0% StdDev=11.4%
   S=33.3 B=24.1 R=33.2 G=9.4

The Super Efficient Portfolio Frontier

1.	A=4	S=36.8	B=31.8	R=38.5	G=24.0	TB=(-31)
	A=12	S=12.3	B=10.6	R=12.8	G=8.0	TB=56

See EFFPORT for answers without the risk free asset.

2.	A=4	S=38.7	B=31.1	R=36.9	G=(-37.3)	TB=31
	A=12	S=12.9	B=10.4	R=12.3	G=(-12.4)	TB=77

In both cases, you are short selling gold.

3.	S=26.54	B=37.89	R=30.57	G=5.0	
	S=12.35	B=10.56	R=12.75	G=5.0	TB=59.35
4.	S=15	B=85	R=0.00	G=0.00	
	S=21.51	B=85	R=1.32	G=9.59	TB=(-17.41)

Index Models & Performance

1. The Sharpe measures are -0.06, -0.03, 0.53, 5.09

Bond Risk Analysis

1.	Bond 1	2.42,	101.92,	5.63%
	Bond 2	3.19,	104.69,	5.95%
	Bond 3	3.13,	104.60,	6.21%
	Bond 4	2.71,	106.68,	6.42%

2. Current $7,028; After 1% rise = $ 6,757
3. Current = (-$138) Hedge 1 = (-$137) Hedge 2 = (-$58)
4. Short sell Hedge portfolio #1
5. Bond 1 = 15 Bond 2 = 19 Bond 3 = 19 Bond 4 = 27

Term Structure

1.

a. The longer the maturity, the larger the spread between duration and maturity.

b. Higher YTM causes lower durations.

c. Higher duration corresponds to higher volatility, which imply that higher duration bonds are more sensitive to interest rate changes.

d. Duration, which measures the average timing of cash flows on a present value basis, varies with YTM. Higher YTM cause duration to drop, resulting in less volatility in bond prices. Since the future represents uncertainty, a drop in duration (or maturity) should lead to reduced uncertainty (or volatility).

2.

a. The two look similar.

b. Each graph indicates a drop in YTM at the end of the term structure. Also, bond #9 has an unexplained drop in yield.

c. The 7.5% coupon bond has a lower duration because you get your money sooner compared to the 6.5% bond. If you get your money sooner, there is less risk. Less risk translates into lower yields.

Quick Bond Valuation

1. \$1,142.36; d = 9.69; md = 9.10; c = 0.30
2. \$1,091.96; Modified duration declines as rates rise.

3. Duration drops, while convexity remains constant. Convexity is less sensitive to interest rate changes than duration. Convexity is, in fact, dropping at a negligible rate relative to duration.
4. Price = \$1,12.96 YTM = 6.70%
5. They are inversely related.
6. up, down, down

Valuing Convertible Debt

1. Non-callable convertibles
2. Call, Convertible
3. When the value of the callable convertible equals its conversion value.
4. Try a theoretical change.
   a. CASH
   b. Total Liabilities after call = \$155.07.
   c. SHARES, TL after call = \$400.
   d. V=\$446, BG=O

The Two-Dividend Growth Model

1. \$ 42.99
2. \$42.32 (If you calculate the answer by hand or with a financial calculator, you may get an answer of \$ 39.64. The difference relates to the computer's

ability to perform certain compounding calculations, which are not feasible when done manually.)

3. Low = $ 38.30 High = $ 48.98

Futures Pricing

1. 1.11%, Prices = 905, 912, 926
2. Various answers possible.
3.
   a. futures prices rise
   b. futures prices rise
   c. futures prices drop

   Futures prices represent forecasted prices. If actual prices and interest rates rise, this should lead to a rise in forecasted prices (futures). Dividends have the opposite effect. Futures rise by more than 3%.
4.
   a. Value rises
   b. Value drops
   c. Value drops

   A 3% rise in the index causes a $11,250 rise in the hedged position and a $67,350 rise in the non-hedged position.
5. Profit = $20,879.73 or $10,984.41
6. Value changes high = $19,853 loss low = $49,275 loss

7. The futures price is above the spot price, but the spread decreases as time passes.

Hedging Dynamics

1. 0.44, 0.56
2. 1, 0
3. Every simulation will differ. Typically, the optimal hedge (bonds and the inflation index) will track the stock index most closely.
4. Again, every simulation will differ.

Options Risk Analysis

1. The April 130 Put seems to be seriously underpriced. Let's assume that gross arbitrage opportunities like this do not arise; perhaps the option hasn't traded for a while, or the newspaper made a typographical error. A more reasonable price might be $16.75, which is assumed for the remainder of the exercise. Implied volatilities for the calls range from 18.4% to 24.5%. You should find the implied volatilities for the entire set of options traded.
2. Strategy (a) loses $1005, (b) gains $39, and (c) loses $541. What happens to the risk factors?
3. The correct tables have the following entries: July 110 Put Vega goes from 0.24 to 0.23; April 120 Put Delta goes from -0. 80 to -0. 83.
4. At the current stock price level, volatility can only drop in order to yield us a profit. At the current volatility level, the stock price must rise, but not above $129 to break even.

Margin Account Simulator

1. Small changes in futures prices translate into large margin account changes.
2. The futures price drops and a loss in value occurs. The loss in value is deducted from the margin account. When the amount in the margin account represents less than 5% of the total position value, a margin call occurs.

Quick European Option Pricing

1. See an investments text book.
2. Call=$1.309 Intrinsic Value = 0 Time premium = $1.309
   Put=$4.801 Intrinsic Value = $4.00 Time premium = $0.801
3. $5,669.13
4. —
   a. Value falls as volatility rises because a covered call has limited upside and significant downside potential. Thus, higher volatility increases the probability of being "deeper" into the loss range.
   b. $5,922.94. The maximum potential value of $6,199.66 occurs at expiration.
5. Delta = 0.323; + $0.251
6. Kappa = 0.084; +$0.085
7. Call price drops; Put price rises

8. Implied volatility = 33.12%

    a. $610.98

    b. The straddle position profits from large swings (up or down) in the stock price.

    c. A $10 drop causes value = $ 1,355.59; A $10 rise causes value = $ 801.85